Musical activities with young children

Jean Gilbert

Ward Lock Educational

ISBN 0 7062 3462 6

First published 1975

Set in 11 on 12 point Plantin
by Woolaston Parker Ltd, Leicester
for Ward Lock Educational
116 Baker Street, London W1M 2BB
Printed in Great Britain
by Robert MacLehose & Co. Ltd
Printers to the University of Glasgow

Contents

Acknowledgments

The ideas presented in this book have materialized over many years of working with children, both in and out of school. Like so many other teachers, I have been influenced by the ideas and work of Carl Orff. The BBC radio and television programmes have been a continual source of stimulating ideas. I am especially grateful to John Hosier whose programmes have provided so much brilliant teaching support and have undoubtedly influenced my approach. I am also indebted to Wendy van Blankenstein, guitarist and singer, with whom I gave hundreds of teaching demonstrations in junior and infant schools, and to Florence Read, at present principal of the Leonide Massine School of Ballet in West Germany, with whom I worked closely when we gave practical lectures in music and movement to nursery nurses.

I would like to thank my friends and colleagues who have read the manuscript of this little book, and particularly the members of my family who have read, discussed and criticized it, and offered technical advice and help in its presentation.

The author and publisher wish to thank Miss Wendy van Blankenstein for permission to reproduce *Paddling in the puddles*, *See the rain come pouring down* and her adaptation of *Oh dear, what can the matter be?*; Mrs J. King for the use of her verse *I am as happy as can be*; and to the following for permission to reprint material in their copyright:

A. and C. Black *High and low*, *Fast and slow* by Peggy Noble, *My motor is humming* by Mona Swann, *Pitter-patter* by W. Kingdon-Ward and *Ring the bell*, all taken from *Speech Rhymes* edited by Clive Sansom; Bosworth and Company Ltd, Martin Schneider and Jack Fishman, *Thank you for giving me this morning* from *Faith Folk and Clarity* edited by Peter Smith and published by Galliard; Doubleday and Company *Train is a-coming Oh-Yes* from *American Folk Songs for Children* by Ruth Seeger; Durand et Cie, Paris *Little Johnny Puppet* from *Anthologie des Chants Populaires Français*, Volume 1 by Cantaloube; Faber Music Limited on behalf of J. Curwen and Sons Limited *When you beat on the Drum* from *Thirty Folk Settings for Children* by Anne Mendoza and Joan Rimmer; Harrap and Company *The Puffer Train* from *Music for the Nursery School* by Linda Chesterman; Oxford University Press *Summer, goodbye* by Frances B. Wood from *Sixty Songs for Little Children*; Penguin Books Limited and Elizabeth Matterson *Down by the station*, *Five currant buns*, *Five little ducks*, *Five little mice*, *Here comes a big red bus*, *John Brown had a little Indian*, *Peter hammers with one hammer*, *Ten fat sausages sitting in the pan*, *The wheels on the bus go round and round*, all taken from *This Little Puffin* by Elizabeth Matterson; Pitman Publishing *The music makers* from *Listen to the Band* by M. Cobby and I. M. Warner; Stainer and Bell *Here comes a policeman riding on his bicycle* from *Echo and Refrain Songs* by E. Barnard, and *Pray open your umbrella* from *Fingers and Thumbs* by Ann Elliott.

Foreword

This book reflects some of the exciting developments in primary school music during the last few years. It also recognizes the new problems and challenges in infant teaching that social changes and investigations into child development have thrown up.

Infant teachers have often pioneered classroom approaches that have later percolated through to the heights of the secondary school. I remember, a few years ago, a school in a fairly tough area of south-east London, where a large class of top infants was working on a space project. One group was preparing a large papier mâché representation of the surface of the moon, another was modelling a space craft, two or three children were writing a story, and in a corner the music group was recording some space music. This took the form of a conducted improvisation: some children were playing classroom percussion instruments, others were using 'found' sounds, like slowly-deflated balloons, water poured from a jug, corks pulled from bottles. One child was playing back sounds they had already recorded onto another tape recorder with various distortions. The conductor was a seven year old who brought in the various sounds, combined them and shut them up. The children in this class explored the sound world of their environment by taking a cassette recorder outside and recording the sounds of the neighbourhood. They would then play the sounds they had recorded in class, discuss them and then play them at different speeds to discover new aspects of them, dramatic, mysterious, funny.

Children were learning to explore their surroundings and to use their discoveries as a basis for stimulating their imagination and creativity. The results were not always beautiful to listen to — but if these results are considered the waste product of an essential process, they are seen in their true perspective.

Children coming to school in nursery and reception classes today are probably unaware of the heritage of nursery rhymes, singing games and finger play that we of an older generation seemed to grow up with. Our infants are much more likely to grow up with the top twenty or television jingles. Children, particularly those in urban areas, come from aurally polluted atmospheres. Musical education must help them discriminate between sounds, and learn to listen anew.

This book takes account of many of the new approaches to music education: it makes useful suggestions about listening awareness through games and play, it has a number of useful activities with songs and singing games, it makes suggestions for developing creativity. It takes into consideration the pitch-percussion instruments now available to schools and also the home-made ones which are proving so useful. There are suggestions about developing children's pitch sense through singing patterns derived from Kodaly and Orff. And it recognizes that broadcasting can be a useful tool.

The book will be of great use to the musically inexperienced teacher. Mrs Gilbert has herself been an imaginative teacher of music in several primary schools and presents a number of approaches from

which teachers can select those that most appeal to
their own temperaments and relate most to the needs
of their children.

John Hosier
March 1975

1 Introduction

The child begins to learn the moment he is born and when he leaves his mother for the first big adventure of nursery, playgroup or reception class, he has already acquired the beginnings of many skills, he has built up a great deal of factual knowledge, and his continuous curiosity about everything within sight, smell and touch is enabling him to come to terms with his environment.

His needs are basically simple; security, stimulating but ordered surroundings, and a teacher who will cater for his physical, emotional and intellectual development. Of course, we know that in practice it is not so straightforward as that, nor can we wrap up the business of educating the young child quite so neatly. Many of us in our teaching are influenced by the kind of things we like and can do best. This is only natural, but do we leave out essential areas in the overall development of the child? I have yet to see a classroom for young children without books, puzzles, number, counting and sorting apparatus, dressing-up corner, paper, paints, toys, a Wendy house or home-play area. But corners of interest where a child can go to experiment with sound, and to make sound, are more often hard to find. Perhaps we feel there is enough sound in the room without providing for more, or perhaps we mistakenly feel that because we can't play an instrument or sing very well we just cannot 'do' music, as it is called, in the curriculum.

But everyday sounds are a vital part of the young child's world: he listens to the wind and rain, clocks ticking, birds and traffic; he hears music from the radio, television, even in the supermarket. A world without sound is dead.

This book is about sound: it is to do with developing the child's musical skills and contains many ideas of how to start. You may need to adapt them to your particular style of teaching; you may decide that some ideas are too advanced, or in some way unsuitable for your group of children. Remember too, that some ideas are compressed; that whereas one group will happily sing little question and answer songs, will enjoy playing in small informal groups and will even cope with the chimes, another group of children will need far longer in the individual experimental stage. Observe your children carefully and then decide what you can do and when you can do it.

Although this book has been written with the nursery and reception class in mind, lots of the songs are sung in playgroups and by children at home, and many of the ideas and suggestions for making and enjoying music can be followed by playgroup leaders and by mothers with their children. It is anticipated that this book will also provide ideas for teachers of middle and top infants: the suggestions contained in many sections are compressed and their development can extend over several years.

2 The beginnings

Sound and rhythm

As soon as the baby begins to move and control his own body, he begins to explore his environment. He touches everything and sucks what he can put into his mouth. His hands and his mouth become the all-important 'feelers'. His exploration of the environment leads him to the banging stage—he claps his hands, hits the table with spoons, plays with his rattles, and later the delighted—if exhausted—parents give him toy drums (something to be avoided in the classroom!). Later still blowing instruments like toy trumpets and mouth organs appear on the scene and the family are subjected to long sessions of constant 'blows', often unrhythmic, all on the same note.

In his desire to explore sound and sound-making materials, the child will spend endless time and seek out many different types of material. Many children have not had such tolerant and resourceful parents, and when they come to the nursery or reception class you, the teacher, must provide for this aspect of their needs. How do you do this, and how do you begin to develop children's rhythmic activities?

One of the first jobs is to ensure that there are plenty of opportunities for the child to make sounds and to listen to them; the atmosphere should be informal, inviting and unhurried, because before he can make sounds with a group and under someone else's direction (in 'percussion' group) he must first of all have had plenty of experience of producing his own sound and finding his own rhythm.

Have a little box in a corner, or a table, for keeping interesting sound-making materials such as walnut shell halves, coconut shells (see section on making simple instruments), little bells, rhythm sticks (only sticks made safe by sand-papering and rounding the ends), and variations on the rattle or shaker. The child himself will doubtless add more bits—a plastic saucer or part of a toy might appear—for all materials are sources for new sounds when discovered by the absorbed experimenter.

A good idea is to fill two or more identical containers with different materials to produce varying sounds. Two fillers that are of sufficient contrast to start with are small corks and rice. If you use transparent containers there's no problem about 'What *is* inside, please open it Miss'. Then you can try using the same filler in different containers. There's no end to the many different sounds that can be produced from shakers.

Bring sound into story time. Many stories lend themselves to sound effects. Sometimes the children will love to join in. Here is one example:
The Three Billy Goats Gruff You could use walnut shell

halves for little Billy Goat Gruff, sticks for middle-sized Billy Goat Gruff and coconuts for big Billy Goat Gruff crossing the bridge, and a big noisy clap for the Troll falling into the water (a recorded splash, or even pour water into a bowl!) Or you could get the children's ideas for the three goats—they might be even better!

If you want to turn it into a joining-in session, let three children play the instruments with the others joining in in groups with fingernail clicking for the little goat, finger clapping for the middle-sized goat and hand clapping for the big goat.

Try making up your own stories with special sound effects—domestic sounds; different kinds of bells; traffic sounds; animal sounds. Have your own collection of sound effects. I have a marvellous bird whistle and a small box that sounds like a real cow when it is inverted! A metal bar or copper tubing makes a good church chime—strike it with a spoon.

Sound is the child's own voice too. He gurgles, coos, cries to begin with. Which mother does not know the difference between a pain cry and an 'I want' cry! Later on he learns to cluck, hiss, hum, imitate others, and gradually to speak and sing.

When he first comes to school he will still be busy absorbing correct pitch relationships. The more the child is sung to and encouraged to sing, the more his sense of pitch will develop—it's as simple as that. Rhythm is part of speech, so for the child, singing involves the development of two skills simultaneously. It is important to remember that he will tend to concentrate on one thing at a time. It may be the rhythm of the words—Humpty Dumpty sat on a wall —it may be the downward bend in the tune of 'The clock struck one, the mouse ran down', or it may be just the fun thing of 'pop' in 'Pop goes the weasel'. It may be some time before he is singing a recognizable

tune. Children's vocal abilities vary enormously, but they all need plenty of opportunity to listen to singing; they all need time to themselves to sing in their own way on their own. Who has not heard the long muttering sessions of an absorbed toddler, or the little tune on two or three notes sometimes to nonsense words, repeated over and over again?

Children love the rhythm of words: they will enjoy just that long before they understand their meanings. 'Doctor Foster went to Gloucester . . .' 'Hey diddle diddle, the cat and the fiddle . . .' They have far more control over their voices than over their limbs and can produce a rhythm like 'Humpty Dumpty sat on a wall' far more easily vocally than by clapping or by skipping —the control of specific body movements comes much later in most children.

When the child is ready to join in with small groups, he begins to develop the skill of keeping in time, in time with *others*. Although children vary in their natural rhythm, they need to acquire the habit of keeping in time if they are going to enjoy any form of music-making with others. This is where finger plays, action songs and singing games are especially valuable because the child can both see and hear the rhythm as he joins in. When you are taking such a group be sure to follow the time and pitch of the children. Take your cues from them. There are lots of good books to help you, and one of the most useful is *This Little Puffin of Finger Plays and Nursery Games* compiled by Elizabeth Matterson (1970). Many more are listed at the back of the book.

3 Development

This chapter consists of a number of sections outlining the many different approaches and types of activity that are possible in a nursery or reception class and in other classes in the infant school. Movement has not been covered because it is a very special area and many excellent books on music and movement are already available (such as *Music Movement and Mime for Children* Gray and Percival [1969], and *Listening and Moving* Carnie [1967]).

Use this chapter for ideas that suit the immediate needs of your children, and when browsing bear in mind possible development of these and make a note of suggestions for later on. Do not attempt too much all at once: you will get indigestion and your children will experience a sense of failure. The most effective use of this chapter depends upon the judgment you must make of the level at which you can teach.

Musical games

Children love playing games; it is a natural way of learning and a very good way of teaching. Games can be used as a 'gatherer' or, when used as part of an informal percussion session, they can provide another way of starting or finishing. Here are a few ideas: I am sure you can think of many more.

Sound games

1   Start with everyday sound objects like a whistle, a teacup and spoon, a clock, a paper bag, etc. Make sure the children have handled them, talked about them, used them, and incorporate them in some of your stories. One day collect them together with a small group of children. Make a sound. Ask a child to make the same sound. Next time hide the objects—in a box, behind a screen, under a cover: get your helper or another (older) child to make a sound. The children can take it in turns to identify and repeat the sound.

2   Have the same or similar set of everyday objects plus pictures of them. Let the child identify the sound by pointing to the picture. Another day play the same game but hide the objects and display the pictures. The children must immediately link the sound with the symbol.

3   Have a set of about three well contrasted instruments (shaker, drum, clapper). Give a duplicate set to a child or a small group. You play one instrument and ask one of the children to play the *same* instrument. Make the game more difficult the next time by adding to each set, and then later by asking the child to imitate

the *way* you are playing on the *same* instrument. Add variety by using sounds like a spoon in a teacup, two blocks of wood, a piece of material or paper, and so on.

4   This same game can be played a different way by hiding both sets of instruments. This means that the child will have to rely much more upon aural discrimination. Hide one set behind a screen or curtain. When you have made a sound, the child must go behind the screen or curtain, identify the source of the sound, and make the same sound. The game can be made more difficult for older children by increasing the instruments or materials used and by choosing sounds that are similar but not identical.

5   Use a screen or cover again. Play *two* instruments at once. Let the one child identify both sounds. Later on just ask the children whether they heard one or two sounds. Sometimes include a chime bar among the instruments. Later on play the game 'is it one or two?' with chime bars.

6   Record some sounds at home (see chapter 5) like a clock ticking, a tap running, a telephone ringing (this involves the cooperation of a friend), a dog barking, doorbell ringing, door shutting. The children must guess what the sounds are.

Record a *sequence* of sounds like tap running, washing-up, water draining away; or alarm clock ringing, brushing teeth, eating cornflakes, footsteps and front door shutting. Can the children identify the sounds and then remember the sound sequence? Can they suggest what might be happening? Let them act out their ideas when you replay the tape, either straightaway or another time.

Clapping games
The hands are the first natural percussive instrument. Always encourage as much rhythmic clapping as possible then clapping games can be fun and more spontaneous. Remember too that a great deal of vocal patterning needs to have been done before you can expect the child to respond rhythmically with his body.

1   Sing and clap with the children a well-known song like 'I hear thunder', then clap a phrase from the song that has a marked rhythm pattern like 'pitter patter raindrops' and ask the children which bit you clapped.

2   If you have nursery rhyme pictures, display two, and sing and clap them through with the children. Clap one of them: the children must guess which one. With older children try three pictures.

3   Try to do plenty of 'echo' clapping. It is best to begin with word association—clap and whisper the words:

Hallo	♩ ♩	Mary	♩ ♩
Goodbye	♩ ♩	Jennifer	♫ ♩
Shut the door	♫ ♩	Christopher	♫ ♩
Yes thank you	♩ ♫	John	♩

One clap is represented by the symbol

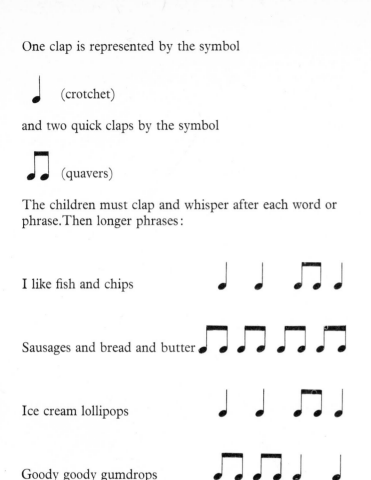

♩ (crotchet)

and two quick claps by the symbol

♫ (quavers)

The children must clap and whisper after each word or phrase. Then longer phrases:

I like fish and chips

Sausages and bread and butter

Ice cream lollipops

Goody goody gumdrops

See if one of the children can think of something to clap for *you* to echo. With older children who have had plenty of practice clapping word patterns, begin clapping rhythms without words for the children to echo. Beats are usually grouped in 2s or 3s or 4s and when clapping it is best to keep to these groupings:

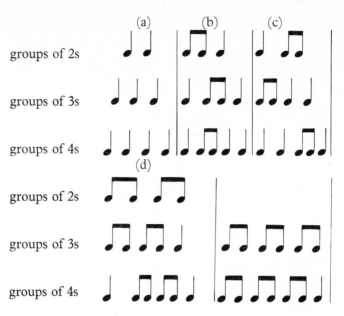

groups of 2s   (a)   (b)   (c)

groups of 3s

groups of 4s

(d)

groups of 2s

groups of 3s

groups of 4s

Begin with the one beat bar (a) and then change only *one* of those beats the next time (b). You may have to practise this by yourself first or with a friend, taking care to keep the beat steady.

Next comes the 'Simon Says' kind of game and again only for the older children who have done lots of echo clapping. The only difference to the last game is that if you clap the same rhythms twice, the children *don't* clap back on the repeat, otherwise they are 'out'. e.g.

teacher   children

1

2

3   no clap (repeat of 2)

13

These little clapping games only last a few minutes, sometimes seconds to begin with, and can provide variety and stimulation within a longer music session. The development outlined here is very condensed and it may take two, even three, years before you can enjoy games like 'Simon says'.

Leaving words out
Sing a well-known song and pretend to forget the last word. Start with leaving out the words that rhyme, like:

Twinkle twinkle little star
How I wonder what you . . . .

Mary Mary quite contrary
How does your garden grow
With silver bells and cockle shells
And pretty maids all in a . . . .

Progress to leaving out the last word in every line. This is excellent for prereading, aural discrimination and recall.

Echo tunes
1   Tell the children how mountains and tunnels 'echo' —how it is just the sound bouncing off the mountains or sides of the tunnel and coming back. You could link this game with a story. Then call some names and let the children echo back—they have to sing exactly what you sing otherwise it isn't a proper echo. Start with the notes of the cuckoo call—chimes G and E as this is one of the most natural pitch sequences for children:

Ma — ry	Tea — time	Jo na than
G E	G E	G G E

Then try longer calls like:

Hurry up
C' C' C'
Don't be long
  G C' G
Daddy's coming home
G   A   G A G — E
(C' means the note C one octave above middle C.)

2   Chime bar echoes: Start with two chime bars, say G and E. Play one of them, then let the child play the same one. Progress to playing two notes—does the child choose the right one to start with? Then try a three-note tune like G E G or G E E or E E G or E G E. The next step is to hide the chimes with a large piece of cardboard so that the child has to rely upon aural discrimination when he comes to the echo. Another way is to have two sets of chimes. If you are part of a school you could borrow the extra set for a morning or afternoon. Be careful not to arrange the sets opposite one another as the tendency may be to mirror the chimes and not necessarily copy the tune! It is best to cover up your set.

3   Talking drums: Play with one or two children. Each has a drum and plays it with hands. Take it in turns to 'speak'. The others must echo what has been 'said'. You could start with names and then everyday conversation like 'Hallo'; 'Good morning'; 'Goodbye'; 'Shut the door'. Progress to snippets of songs or poems that they know: 'Pitter-patter raindrops'; 'Pop goes the weasel!'

The music corner
Ideally the place set aside and prepared for 'sound' play should be in one of the quietest areas of the

classroom. This is not always possible; indeed sound spills over into all areas of the infant and nursery classroom. However, as with sand play, water play and home play, there should be a special place for sound play and, as with the other areas, it should be made exciting and stimulating. This involves careful thought, preparation and daily supervision. With larger classes it will involve rules like restricting the number of children using the corner at any one time, and possibly the withdrawal of its use at certain times of the day like story time.

You will not be treated to continuous 'jam' sessions if you select carefully the instruments and materials for the children to use, and if you take an interest in what goes on. Don't cover the table with too many instruments: put out about two of each variety and occasionally withdraw the lot in order to highlight a particular activity. Display suitable pictures and change them when necessary. Here are a few ways of structuring the use of the music corner:

1   Leave out a number of shakers that are different in appearance, size and sound: which is the biggest, smallest, loudest, softest? Compare the sounds made by the biggest and the smallest; compare the sizes of the loudest and softest instrument.

2   Leave out a set of shakers that are identical in appearance, but whose fillings produce different sounds (cork, sand, rice, stones, nails, marbles). It is essential for the child to be able to see the contents, so transparent containers are vital.

3   Leave out a set of different sized and shaped containers with the same filling. Again, use transparent containers.

4   Leave out a variety of instruments—drums, coconut shells, soft shakers, sand blocks. Which one would they use for:

	Suggested tune
a soldier marching	Grand Old Duke of York
a pony trotting	Yankee Doodle
a lullaby for a baby	Hush a bye baby
a wriggly worm	Under a stone where the earth was firm
	I found a wriggly wriggly worm.

5   Leave out chime bars E and G for tune making. This idea is developed in the section on activities with percussion and chimes.

6   Leave out suitable chimes for playing tunes or parts of tunes by ear. See also the section on activities with percussion and chimes.

Use the music corner to develop language. Ask the child questions or get him to explain to you what he is doing. Observe him carefully so that you can guide him and not direct him. Try a few 'sound' experiments:

1   Jane is playing a rubber drum. Can she tell you what she does to get a loud sound. 'Play loudly' she will probably reply; then ask her to say how she plays. Can she tell you how she plays softly?

See if Jane has observed what happens to the drum itself when it is banged. Let her put her fingers lightly on the top while you bang it. She will feel the rubber *vibrate*—a new word for her! Sprinkle a little sand on the rubber and let her watch it dance up and down while she plays. Observe with her the different ways the sand moves when the drum is played loudly, then softly.

2   When the chime bars are out, discuss the difference in sizes with the children. Why are they different: does the difference relate to the sound? Take low C and high C. Get the children to describe the difference in size and then in sound. Take two more notes. Can they say which is higher by looking at it? If you have the complete scale C D E F G A B C', arrange the chimes in order. Let the children hear the musical *scale*—another new word. Count the notes as you play them. Pretend to climb a ladder. Where does the sound come from? What happens if you strike the chime bar and then put your finger on it? Strike a triangle and see if the sound stops when it is touched.

3   If you have a recorder, play to the children. Play a few notes slowly. Ask them how you can get different sounds. They will observe that you move your fingers. With older children you can talk about the column of air being shorter or longer.

4   Use a one-stringed guitar to demonstrate pitch on a string (see chapter 4) or, if you can play a guitar, show them on your instrument.

Some background to these experiments is given in chapter 6, in the section 'Hearing a sound'.

Activities with percussion and chime bars

Percussion
Here are some ways of making little 'sound' pictures.

The children will have been experimenting in this direction on their own or with a friend. When the opportunity occurs, help them to build on their own discoveries.

1   A rainy day
The children go out with their mothers to the park, but it begins to rain. They put on their coats and hurry home as the rain gets heavier. They listen to the rain on the windows when they get home. Afterwards the house and the garden are dripping wet. Then the sun comes out.

Instruments (after discussion with the children):

rain	shakers, bells, triangles
footsteps	clappers, sticks, drums
rain on the windows and drips	tapping of a 'damped' triangle or chime bar
sun coming out	gentle chimes (any tune)

This could start as a story, or observations of the weather. The children will begin by trying out sound effects on different instruments. Then let them choose which particular sound they would like to make. Explain the 'sound' story and you conduct with the children sitting around you. Point to the child or children when it is their turn to play, indicating soft, loud or graduated sounds, and stopping and starting. You will soon evolve your own conducting signals.

This idea could lead to a little dramatic movement with some of the children accompanying on their instruments.

Rhymes
Rain rain go away
Come again another day

Doctor Foster went to Gloucester
In a shower of rain;
He stepped in a puddle
Right up to his middle
And never went there again.

Pitter-patter,
Pitter-patter,
Listen to the rain!
Pitter-patter,
Pitter-patter,
On the window pane!

Rain on the house-top,
Rain on the tree,
Rain on the green grass—
But don't rain on me!

Songs
Paddling in the puddles
Paddling in the puddles
Paddling in the puddles
But don't let mummy see (*whisper*)

See the rain come pouring down,
Cleaning up the dirty town,
Filling all the gutters full,
As the children go to school.
(To the tune of '*In and out the windows*')
Make up another verse of your own.

Pray open your umbrella,
Pray open your umbrella,
Pray open your umbrella,
And shield me from the rain.

The shower is nearly over,
The shower is nearly over,
The shower is nearly over,
So shut it up again.

2   A thunderstorm
This idea should follow a thunderstorm and let the
children work out their excitement, or fear. They will
be obsessed by the noise of the thunder, the big thunder
claps, the sound of the wind and rain, and the sight of
the lightning flashes. What an opportunity for language
development too!

Instruments (after discussion with the children):
thunder   rubber drums or a rumble on the piano bass,
           clappers for the bangs
lightning (if you *can* portray this sound) a rasp or
           guiro or wooden washboard is effective.
           Maybe just a hard strike on a triangle or
           piece of copper tubing
wind   voices
rain   shakers, bells, triangles, or trills on the piano
           treble

Talk about how a thunderstorm starts, develops, and
gradually peters out. Let the children practise playing
loudly, softly, *getting* louder and *getting* softer. How
would they portray heavy hail or tiny raindrops? Sit
the children around you and conduct them with hand
signals.
This idea could become part of the Noah's Ark
story, using 'The animals went in two by two'.

Songs
I hear thunder—see page 22 and 30.
(See also songs and rhymes for 'A rainy day')

17

3 Fireworks

This is mainly an idea for November, but it can follow the excitement of any firework display the children have experienced. The children's ideas for representing the sound and visual effects of the fireworks will no doubt be quite different from mine, but here are some suggestions:

rocket	sand block and/or shakers for the initial launch and bells or chimes for the coloured lights that float down
jumping jack	clappers
bangers	anything that bangs
sparklers	triangles, chimes, bells
golden rain	gentle shakers
catherine wheel	sand block and/or shakers with chimes

A swanee whistle makes a good '*wheee*' for general effect.

Sit the children round you and let them practise their instruments individually: encourage critical listening. Then conduct a fireworks session. Try to get the impression of a gradual build up of movement and sound, of a show of rockets for instance, and then a slowing down of activity at the end. Start with one player, then add a few more; then fireworks stopping and starting all the time. Stop them gradually until you have one jumping jack left.

This is a very good basis for a movement session accompanied by percussion—it could spark off some colourful paintings.

4 Trains

The magic of trains never palls even though they are no longer a common mode of transport. Children chuff happily away behind a leader, acting out the life of the elusive train. However, after holidays come the little bits of newsy chatter and perhaps the spark of a train will be heard at the music corner. So here are some extension ideas:

the train	shakers, sand blocks, bells, scrapers
whistle	just that—most important!
the guard	a child

The main thing about train sounds is that they are rhythmic. Try to think of some words like chuffa-chuffa, chuffa-chuffa, with a good accent on the first 'chuff'. Get all the children to practise whispering the words and playing their instruments very rhythmically. Practise getting gradually faster and then gradually slower. Then introduce the whistle and the guard calling 'Right away there now!'

Trains don't always go in a direct line from one station to the next. Discuss with the children what else they do—go up hills and down, through tunnels, and sometimes stop at level crossings. Then conduct your group getting the graduations in speed, the tunnel with the whistle, the starting and the stopping.

This idea transfers well to movement with one group of children being the train, tunnel, guard, driver and signal, and the second group making the sounds. Make sure you change over afterwards!

Story books
The Little Red Engine series by Diana Ross is ideal, but there are many more. Make one up and introduce sound effects.

Songs
Puffer train, puffer train,
Noisy little puffer train.

18

If you're going to the sea
Puffer train, oh please take me.
ch . . .   .
Noisy little puffer train.

Down by the station, early in the morning
See the little puffer trains all in a row.
See the engine driver pull the little handle
Choo, choo, choo, and off we go.

This Little Puffin is a good source for more songs and
rhymes; also *American Folk Songs for Children*, edited by
Ruth Seeger, for example:
1   Train is a-coming—Oh-yes
2   Better get your tickets—Oh-yes
3   Going past the signal—Oh-yes
4   Stopping at the station—Oh-yes

5   The high road
Town children especially will be alert to traffic and city
sounds. Get them to tell you what sounds they hear
when they go shopping with their mothers, or go out
with them one day and listen. Take a tape recorder!
Here are some ideas:

bicycle	bell is possible or trill a triangle
ambulance	chimes C and A
lorry	shakers plus voice for air brakes
pedestrians	clappers
ice-cream van	chimes
motor-bike	scrapers
cars	different variety of shakers played by tapping them
policeman	whistle

You could make a sound picture of what the
policeman hears on a crossroad at traffic lights, or
relate to the situation in your area. Always get the
children to sit around you and practise their sounds
individually first. Then decide on the pattern of the
group composition and conduct accordingly. You could
sometimes try letting a child conduct. Make junk models
of all the vehicles. Make a collage of a street scene.

Songs
The wheels on the bus go round and round
Round and round, round and round.
The wheels on the bus go round and round
All day long.

Here comes a policeman riding on a bicycle
Ting, ling, ling, keep the roadway clear.
When I am older I shall ride a bicycle,
Ting, ling, ling, keep the roadway clear.

Rhymes
My motor is humming,
I'm coming, I'm coming,
Make room, make room, make room!
Not a minute to wait,
I'm late, I'm late,
Make room, make room, make room!

Here comes a big red bus,
A big red bus, a big red bus,
Here comes a big red bus,
To take us to the shops.

In conclusion
Ideas for sound pictures can start from almost any part
of the classroom, from stories and songs and from the
children's experiences. They can lead on to movement,

dramatic play, art and junk modelling. An important ingredient of the group work is that it should follow some shape or pattern, as indicated by the suggestions attached to these examples. This is one aspect of musical composition that can be introduced even at this early age.

Tune making with chime bars
Let the children have plenty of opportunity for playing the chime bars freely. Leave them in the music corner; include them in informal percussion sessions; use them yourself to play to the children—they will then be more relaxed when they handle them and will consequently be more able to control their playing. Remember to show the children the correct way of playing the chime bars *before* they start to handle them. Discourage a fierce possessive grip on the beater; the arm and wrist should be relaxed so that the beater can bounce off the metal part of the chime bar which should be played in the middle.

One day try an echo game with chimes E and G: research indicates that this is the most common interval used in children's chants and play songs.

1   Whisper and clap rhythmically some of the children's names. The children must echo and clap back immediately after each name:

Jonathan Jonathan

2   Now sing the names and accompany on the two chime bars E and G like this:

teacher	children
Mary	Mary
G E	G E
Jennifer	Jennifer
G G E	G G E
Simon	Simon
G E	G E
Jonathan	Jonathan
G G E	G G E

To begin with use the natural call with the upper note G on the accented syllables (the cuckoo call).

When the children echo the names let them play pretend chime bars. This gives them practice in synchronizing their hand movements with what they are singing, and encourages relaxation. In bigger groups it is a valuable discipline.

3   Let some of the children have a turn at making a tune using their own names. See if you and the other children can sing the echo.

4   Leave the chime bars out in the music corner and watch for developments.

5   Play the chime bar echo game another day using every day conversations like:

Hallo
G E
How are you?
  G G E
Please shut the door
  G   G G E
Here's your mummy
  G   G G E

Keep the shape of the 'cuckoo' tune until the children feel happy with the two chime bars E and G.

6 You could go on to little question-and-answer games substituting the answer for the echo:

Question	What did you have for breakfast?
(with chimes)	G G G G G E
Answer	Corn flakes
(child sings or	G E
teacher helps	Bread and butter
with chimes)	G G G E
	Orange juice
	G G E

Encourage mini-conversations in the music corner. Two sets of chime bars would be useful. Very few of us can double up on the chimes, but it is sometimes possible if you are part of a school and can borrow them for a few half-days.

7 The range of notes for tune making can be extended as the children become skilled with the existing chime bars, but this should be done *very, very gradually*. Add the notes in this order—A D C C'— building up to the pentatonic scale on C: C D E G A C'. The joy of this grouping is that tunes can begin and end on any note and still sound good. But remember that many groups of children will not be ready to work with more than two or three notes until they are much older—top infants, lower juniors—even if they have made a start in their nursery or reception classes. Other groups and some individual children may be ready for the full scale. Be alert to their potential; be flexible in your approach.

8 Further tune making can be based on short verses or rhymes, such as:

Rain rain go away
Come again another day

Chimes	*Percussion*
Ring the bell!	Ting-a-ling-ling!
Knock at the door!	Rat-a-tat-tat!
Draw the latch!	Click-clack!
And walk right in.	

High and low,
Fast and slow—
That is the way
The swing-boats go.

Playing by ear
All children love picking out a tune that they know. Here are several tunes and snippets of tunes that you can try with your children. Introduce them when you are singing or playing with the children and then leave them on the music table with a suitable illustration. It is best to start with tune snippets (see stage 1 of the analysed tunes and the short list at the end of this section). Give the children plenty of variety at this stage and remember to sing the songs from which the snippets have been taken as frequently as you can.

1 *Three blind mice*—Chimes C D E F G A B C'
Stage 1 Three blind mice
       E   D   C
Stage 2 Three blind mice (repeat)
       E   D   C
      See how they run (repeat)
       G F F E
Stage 3 Three blind mice (repeat)
       E   D   C
      See how they run (repeat)
       G F   F E
      They all run after the farmer's wife
    * G C' C' B A B C' G   G
      Who cut off their tails with a carving knife
    * G C' C' C' B   A B C' G   G
      Did ever you see such a sight in your life as
    * G C' C' B A B C' G G G F
      Three blind mice
       E   D   C
      *(Notice the repeat tune)

2 *I hear thunder* (*Frère Jacques*)—
   Chimes C F G A B♭ C' D
Stage 1 I hear thunder
       F G A F
Stage 2 I'm wet through So are you
       F C F   F C F
Stage 3 I hear thunder Hark don't you
       F G A F A B♭ C'

The children can now play the tune right through except for 'Pitter patter raindrops'. Get them to play the shakers, bells or triangle on this bit when they get to it:

Stage 4 (for a few older or more able children)
      I hear thunder (repeat) Hark don't you (repeat)
      F G A F   A B♭ C'
      Pitter patter raindrops (repeat)
      C' D' C' B♭ A F
      I'm wet through So are you
      F C F   F C F

3 *Peas pudding hot*—Chimes G A B C'
Stage 1 Peas pudding hot
       G G A B
Stage 2 Peas pudding hot Peas pudding cold
       G G A B C' C' C' B
Stage 3 (for a few older children)
      Peas pudding hot Peas pudding cold
      G G A B C' C' C' B
      Peas pudding in the pot nine days old
      G G A B B B A A G

4 *Hot-cross buns*—Chimes C F G A B♭ C'
Stage 1 Hot-cross buns
       C' C F
Stage 2 One a penny two a penny Hot-cross buns
       C B♭ A G F G A B♭ C' C F
Stage 3 If you have no daughters
       C' C' C' C' B♭ B♭
      Give them to your sons
      A   A   A A G
Stage 4 A few older children could try the whole tune

5 *London's burning*—Chimes C F G A B♭ C'
Stage 1   London's burning
          C   C   F   F
Stage 2   London's burning (repeat)
          C   C   F   F
          Fetch the engines (repeat)
            G G A   A
Stage 3   Fire! Fire! Fire! Fire!
          C' C' C' C'
Stage 4   Pour on water (repeat)
          C' B♭ A A
Stage 5   Some older children could play the whole tune

This tune could be played by three children:

Child 1   London's burning
Child 2   Fetch the engine
Child 3   Fire! Fire!
Child 2   Pour on water
          (would have to take top C from child 3)

6 *Lavender's blue*—Chimes F G A B♭ C' D'
Stage 1   Lavender's blue
          F C' C'   C'
Stage 2   Lavender's blue, diddle, diddle!
          F C' C'   C'   B♭ A G F
Stage 3   Lavender's green
          F D' D'   D'
Stage 4   When I am King, diddle, diddle!
            F C' C'   C' B♭ A G F
          (same as 2)
          You shall be Queen
            B♭ A   G   F
Stage 5   Some older children could play the tune right
          through .

7 *Summer goodbye*—Chimes F G A B♭ C'
   (alternate chimes C D E F G)
Stage 1   Summer goodbye (repeat)
          A   A G F (E E D C)
Stage 2   Summer goodbye
          A   A B♭ C' (E E F G)
Stage 3   Summer goodbye (repeat)
          A   A G F (E E D C)
Sing the middle bit—Roses their petals shed
                    Apples are turning red
              Summer goodbye Summer goodbye
          A   A B♭ C' A   A G F
          E   E F G E   E D C

8 *This old man*—Chimes C D E F G A
Stage 1   This old man he played one
            G E G G E   G
Stage 2   He played nick-nack on my drum
            A G   F   E D F
Stage 3   Join first two stages together
Stage 4   Nick-nack paddywhack give a dog a bone
            G   C   C   C C D E F G
Stage 5   This old man came rolling home
            G D D   F   E D C
Stage 6   Some older children could try the whole tune.
          This is rather more difficult because of the
          repeated notes and the relative speed of stage
          4, so you might prefer to stick to the first
          stage only.

(This song can be sung at a higher pitch for older
children as shown in the section 'Extending songs'.)

Some snippets
Holy night
GAG E

Cock-a-doodle-doo
  C E E D   E

Baa baa black sheep
  C C G   G

Little Bo-Peep has lost her sheep
  FF   F   F   F G   G   G

Puffer train
C E   G *or*
D F♯ A

Ten green bottles
  F   F   F A

Sur le pont d'Avignon
(On the bridge at Avignon)
  F F F GG G

See-saw Margery Daw
  C' G C' C' C' G

Hickory dickory dock
E F G G A B C'

Jill came tumbling after
  G F E D C C

More about percussion

I suggested in chapter 2 that children should have plenty of opportunity to experiment with sound, and I have described ways of maintaining the interest of the music corner. Don't hurry this stage: there is a lot to be experienced and assimilated. The important thing is that you observe each child and that you lead him a step further when he is ready. At first he may be entirely absorbed by the look and feel of these new 'toys'. He will carry them around and just hold on to them indefinitely, or they will be discarded when his interest is caught by something new. He will use them in his games and in his play: you will introduce them into story time and dramatic play and use them perhaps for movement and with songs.

There will come a time however when some of the children will be ready for the new experience of making music together. Perhaps the activity around the music corner has occasionally developed into a group, the children talking about the sounds they make—comparing, contrasting, imitating, sometimes playing their instruments together. This may be the time for some musical games suggested earlier; you may decide to follow on with an informal percussion session.

Here is one way of starting: have the instruments in the middle of an area, more than enough for the numbers you expect and not too many of the 'loud' variety like clappers. (As a general rule the younger the child the smaller the group needs to be.) Start with the instruments the children have been using in the music corner and limit the variety to begin with, for example with a group of twenty children give

5   a small selection of date-box clappers *or* rhythm
    sticks
10 a larger selection of shakers
5   a selection of rubber drums with beaters (usually
    the whole lot unless you are lucky enough to have
    more than enough) plus extras to avoid squabbling.

1   Let the children choose an instrument and sit in a
circle. They will play as soon as they have picked up
their instrument, so do not delay starting. Just put your
hand up as a 'stop' signal, and accustom them to this.
Then proceed as at 3.

2   Alternatively, with a noisier, larger group, let the
children sit first in a circle, and quietly call their names,
or hold up their name cards for them to choose an
instrument. Then insist on them being clever enough to
'stop their instruments talking' until everyone is ready.

3   Then proceed with hand signals like this. You will,
if it is the first time, have to say what is meant by each
signal:

Everyone play loudly

Everyone stop

Do this several times until the children are used to
keeping their eye on you for stopping.

Everyone play very softly

Everyone stop

Again, do this several times, and then alternate loudly with softly.

Ask groups of instruments to play loudly, stop, softly, stop, or—later—individual children. 'Listen to Janet playing loudly/softly,' etc. Always use the same hand signs.

Everyone play slowly
(move arms up and down slowly)

Everyone stop

Everyone play quickly
(move arms up and down quickly)

Everyone stop

Ask groups of instruments to play slowly/quickly. Then individual children. You can now proceed to:

softly and slowly
softly and quickly
loudly and slowly
loudly and quickly

Make up your own signs for these. Later proceed to:

getting quicker (and louder) (and softer)
getting slower (and louder) (and softer)
getting louder (and quicker) (and slower)
getting softer (and quicker) (and slower)

This graduated movement demands great control. Try one idea first like 'getting quicker', and much later the 'two in one'—'getting quicker and louder' etc.

There is another thing children love doing: they love finding a different sound—playing their instruments in a different way. One will play on the side of his drum, another will reverse the date-box clappers so that the handles click; shakers are very versatile—they can be tapped, gently turned upside-down or rotated. All these ways of playing have probably gone on in the music corner but children love to watch—they get ideas too. So invent a hand signal for 'different sounds', and then get individual children to play. My children never let me miss this one out!

Let the children conduct sometimes: even my shyest ones have been eager to try. But if the eagerness of a shy child turns into embarrassment, quickly help out. With older children I have occasionally tried having two conductors—a girl conducting girls and a boy conducting boys: this has worked well and obviates dividing into groups which slows down the momentum of the session.

4 Finish with one or two songs of contrasting styles that the children know well and like, such as *Baa baa black sheep* and *Twinkle twinkle little star*. Try to get them to vary their playing to fit the song. Or, if you have a tape recorder and have been able to prepare your own short tape of songs (see chapter 5), this is a good way of concluding.

Such a session may only last a few minutes; or it may even last ten to fifteen minutes: but however long there should be a sense of enjoyment and achievement. Don't forget to let the children change over instruments occasionally.

Music cards
When the children are getting more expert at handling the instruments and are used to the discipline of playing with others, start introducing music cards. (These are similar in function to reading flash cards and provide a valuable prereading and number activity. You hold up the card and the children must interpret the instruction and play accordingly.)

1 Start with these cards for all instruments:

front

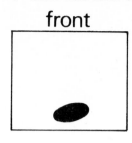

back

front

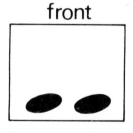

back

Prepare cards for as many numbers as your children know.

Ways of playing

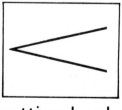

getting louder

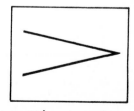

getting softer

**getting louder
then softer**

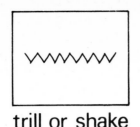

trill or shake

Ways of playing

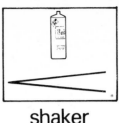

shaker

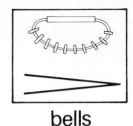

bells

The symbol ● for one beat or strike has been suggested as a preparation for music reading. Help the children at first by pointing to each symbol and remember to move from *left to right*.

2   Later on introduce cards for different groups of instruments.

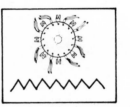

tambourine

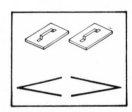

sandpaper blocks

front

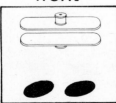

back

3

The children also love to have a turn at holding up the cards. Holding up two sets of cards (boys and girls) can be fun for a very short time if you feel your children are sufficiently ready. Always finish with a short general playing session as suggested in the notes on conducting.

front

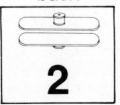

back

2

Extending songs
The ideas attached to each song suggest different ways the song can be approached with children of differing ages and abilities. The important thing is to try simple actions and build on them. Only introduce one new idea at a time and remember your aim is relaxed enjoyment. Never try out anything new if the children are tired or fractious. Only you can judge the right time and feel the response.

The use of the chime bar parts is optional but adds depth to the music making and enjoyment for the older and more able child.

The letters underneath the stave refer to the names of the notes and should enable you to pick out the tune on a piano, glockenspiel or chime bars. C' D' and E' mean high C, high D and high E. The shape of the tune has been indicated in the first three songs.

Hickory Dickory Dock—using notes C D E F G A B C'

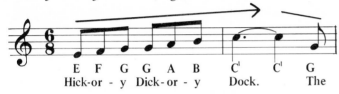

E F G G A B C' C' G
Hick-or - y Dick-or - y Dock. The

E F G G A B C' C' G
mouse ran up the clock. The

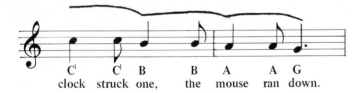

C' C' B B A A G
clock struck one, the mouse ran down.

G A G F E D C
Hick -or - y Dick-or - y Dock.

This is a very good tune for illustrating rising and falling patterns of sound.

1 Pretend the fingers are mice and run up the clock. Clap on 'one' and then run down again with fingers.

2 Pretend to be a clock ticking—hands or body swaying to the 'ticks'. Can you sing at the same time?

3 Get one or two children to 'tick' while the others sing and mime as in 1.

4 Introduce chime bars E and C, for 'tick tock'. Get the children to sing 'tick tock' with chime bars while you quietly sing the tune. You must start on E to make it sound right. Get a child to play E C, while others sing the tune. This can be done if you have left chime bars E and C, on the music table. The children will have had the opportunity to play them on their own. You could pin up a colourful picture of the nursery rhyme by the music corner—or pictures of different clocks.

5 Don't miss the opportunity of talking about clocks some time. Listen with the children to different 'ticks' —your wrist watch, the kitchen clock from the mantelpiece—get one if you can. Do they know what a grandfather clock is? Have they heard about Big Ben? Visit a clock shop.

6 Make a clock and mouse out of a scrap of material (see page 30).

7 Grandfather clock goes   tick   tock
                           (slow) (slow)
  Kitchen clock goes   tick-tock   tick-tock
                      (quick quick) (quick quick)

Mummy's wristwatch   ticker-tocker   ticker-tocker
goes   (quickly quickly) (quickly quickly)

If you feel you can try this, start with the rhythm of
one clock—the grandfather clock. Let the children move
and say the slow beat first, then see if they can hear the
tick of the kitchen clock—you whisper tick tock at twice
the speed. Then change over parts. Another day divide
the children and see if they can pretend to be the two
clocks ticking at the same time in the clock shop. With
older children you can try introducing a third rhythm
starting with you saying the rhythm while two groups
are ticking away at the other two clocks. If the
opportunity occurs and you know the children well, try
using sounds; the children will give you ideas. You
could try sticks for the kitchen clock, finger nails for
the wristwatch (instruments are difficult for this quick
rhythm) and a chime bar for the grandfather clock.

I Hear Thunder—using notes C F G A B♭ C' D'

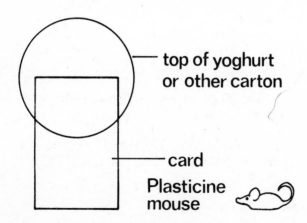

top of yoghurt
or other carton

card

Plasticine
mouse

Many children know this tune as 'Frère Jacques', but in this climate these words are very appropriate, especially on rainy days, or after a thunderstorm, which they often don't talk about if they are frightened. The features of the tune are the repeated phrases—and the 'pitter patter' middle section.

1   Mime the first two lines with hands cupping ears. 'Pitter patter raindrops'—imitate rain coming down with fingers. Mime 'I'm wet through' and point to someone else for 'So are you'.

2   Same but make rain noises on 'pitter patter' with either finger nails, bells, tambourines or two spoons—get ideas from the children.

3   Same but let someone play a drum for 'I hear thunder' or suggest an appropriate loud sound. You now have contrasting sounds made by the children.

4   Try a sound picture of rain. This might start at the sound corner with one or two children, or it could follow the song if you have enough instruments at the ready. Almost any kind of instrument will do, but you need to go easy on the noisier ones with bigger groups. You obviously could not do this with a big reception class of twenty-five or more unless circumstances were ideal (with discipline and help), or unless you had already embarked upon a percussion session (see section on percussion).
Practise playing loudly then softly. Practise *getting* louder and *getting* softer, using suitable hand signs.
Now the thunderstorm—bring children in by pointing. Start with drums and then stop. Now a few shakers or bells for rain beginning: add a few more players, then all together getting louder. Gradually get softer and finish with 'dripping sounds'.

5   Introduce chime bars F and C for someone who would like to play a little tune all on their own. Start with F and play the chimes like this:

F C F C F C F C
I'm wet through So are you

Get everyone to help with this tune: keep repeating it until everyone can sing it—especially the one who is going to play it. Everyone can then play pretend chimes while the real player has a go. This repeated tune sounds nice sung as a background to the song itself. Both tunes start on F.
If your children have had plenty of varied musical experiences try these further ideas:

6   This song can be sung as a round, but only with children who have had plenty of musical background, with an exceptionally musical group or with a mixed group including older children. Divide into two groups. The second group starts when the first group begins 'Hark don't you?' It is useful to have a helper to start rounds off.

7   This idea is quite ambitious, and again for the older or more ambitious children. Start with the F—C tune as described in 5 and keep it going while you sing the round. You will need a reliable child for the tune, and your helper if possible. It's fun, but drop it if it doesn't come off!

8   See also *Playing by ear* (page 21).

Hot Cross Buns—using notes C F G A B♭ C

C' C F C' C F
Hot cross buns Hot cross buns

C' B♭ A G F G A B♭ C' C F
One a pen-ny, two a pen-ny Hot cross buns.

C' C' C' C' B♭ B♭ A A A G
If you have no daugh-ters Give them to your sons.

C' B♭ A G F G A B♭ C' C F
One a pen-ny, two a pen-ny Hot cross buns.

The features of this tune are the repeated phrases for 'Hot cross buns' and 'One a penny two a penny'. The shape of the tunes making up the whole is interesting with the big interval leaps in 'Hot cross buns', the gentle run down and up for 'One a penny two a penny', and the graduated descent for 'If you have no daughters, give them to your sons'. (There is another musical version to this phrase!)

1 This is a jolly good marching tune. Let the children pretend they have a tray of buns on their heads.

2 Let the children clap the rhythm of 'Hot cross buns' (quick, quick, slow) while you sing the tune through.

3 Let one of the children try the tune of 'Hot cross buns' on chime bars C' C F arranged in that order. The difficulty is the long note on F. It helps if the child plays an imaginary chime bar to fill in the time of the long note, and then goes back to C' again. Get all the children to pretend to play the tune.

Try singing 'Hot cross buns' while the chime bars play their tune over and over again.

Leave the chime bars on the music table and try out the idea another day.

4 Try modernizing the words for a baking session:

Fairy cakes! Fairy cakes!
One a penny, two a penny Fairy cakes!
We've been busy making lovely Fairy cakes.
One a penny, two a penny Fairy cakes!

5 See also *Playing by ear* (page 21).

6 A good song to link with this one is 'Five currant buns in the baker's shop' and it dramatizes well if you put in the names of individual children. 'Along came *Mary* with a penny one day'. You then need five children for the currant buns, one for a baker, and five children to each buy a bun! A baker's hat really brings this to life.

Jack and Jill—using notes C D E F G A C' D' E'

G G G G C' C' C' C'
Jack and Jill went up the hill to

D' D' D' D' E' C'
Fetch a pail of wa - ter

G G G G A A A A
Jack fell down and broke his crown and

G F E D C C
Jill came tum - bling af - ter.

This tune is based on the skipping rhythm ♩♪♩♪ (long short long short). There are a lot of repeated notes and a lovely skip down the scale at the end—'Jill came tumbling after'.

1 As a finger play song, let the children climb up the hill with their hands, one on top of the other, to the first line. Give a big clap for 'Jack fell down', put hands on head for 'broke his crown' and tumble hands down into laps for 'Jill came tumbling after'.

2 Let the children act out the story:

Up Jack got and home did trot
As fast as he could caper.
He went to bed to mend his head
With vinegar and brown paper.

When Jill came in how she did grin
To see Jack's paper plaster.
Her mother vexed did whip her next
For causing Jack's disaster.

3 Play a game with the children. Play the tune to 'Jill came tumbling after' on the chime bars. Ask the children to tell you the words that fit the tune, then get them to sing that phrase several times while you play it on the chime bars. Leave the chime bars out on the music table—with an appropriate picture—and encourage the children to try out that little tune.

4 Play the same game another day. Choose a child who has successfully managed the tune in the music corner to come and play it. When continuously repeated, this little tune can accompany the whole song. Try this idea when your helper is with you.

5 Clap the rhythm of 'Jill came tumbling after' with the children. Repeat it slowly and rhythmically. Children find the skipping rhythm difficult to clap especially at speed: they need plenty of practice.

6 Next time the children sing the song, you accompany them on a percussion instrument using the rhythm of 'Jill came tumbling after'. Let one or two of the children play with you.

7 Paint pictures or make models of Jack and Jill.

8 Talk about the well with the children. A good song to link with this idea is 'Ding dong bell, Pussy's in the well'.

c

Songs to use with percussion

A simple beginning to the tune of 'Mulberry Bush'— using notes D E F♯ G A B D'

2 We can play our rubber drums, rubber drums,
    rubber drums
    We can play our rubber drums, boom, boom, boom.
    (Repeat this—first *loudly* and then *softly*.)
3 We can play our shakers gay, etc. Shake, shake, shake.
    (Repeat as before.)
4 We can play our jingle bells, etc. Ting, ring, ring.
5 We can play our tambourines, etc. Chink, chink,
    chink.
6 We can play our castanets, etc. Click, click, click.
7 We can play our instruments, etc. Tra-la-la.

The Music Makers—using notes D E F♯ A B

2 Here are the dainty bells, ring, ring ring, ring ring
    (repeat)
3 Here are the tambourines, clash, clash clash, clash
    clash (repeat)
4 Here are the castanets, click, click click, click click
    (repeat)
5 Here are the shakers gay, shake, shake shake, shake
    shake (repeat)
6 Here are the rubber drums, boom, boom boom,
    boom boom (repeat)

The Band (Traditional)—using notes C D E G A B C'

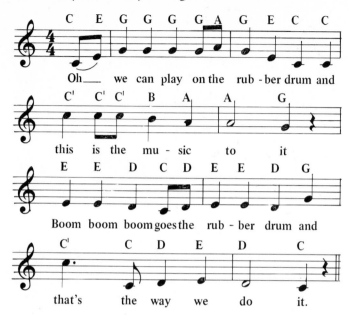

2 Oh we can play on our shakers gay (shake shake shake)
3 Oh we can play on our jingle bells (ting ring ring)
4 Oh we can play on our tambourines (chink chink chink)
5 Oh we can play on our castanets (click click click)
6 Oh we can play on our instruments (tra-la-la)

Let the children sit down first to learn the song and do the actions only. The last two are both good marching songs, so they could on another day march round performing the actions either altogether or in groups, or in groups with a leader playing the instrument. When the song is really wellknown and if the group is not too large, let all the children have

instruments. Start with a few verses and gradually build up.

When you beat on the drum—using notes C D E G A B C'

Teach the song first letting the children mime the actions either sitting down or marching around as suggested for 'The Band'. If you have a child who is particularly good with the chime bars, fit in the chime bar accompaniment as shown. This is very simple. Just top C and bottom C all the way through except for the bar 'all through the' when chime bar G is played.

Little Johnny Puppet—using notes E F♯ G A B♭ (this is the same sound as A♯) B C'

```
Chimes   E    E     E  E    A    A     E    E
         E  B  B A♯  B  G    A A A B    G F♯ E
      1  Lit-tle John-ny dan-ces, On my thumb he dan-ces,

         E    E     E  E    A    A     E    E
         E  B  B A♯  B  G    A A A B    G F♯ E
         Lit-tle John-ny  dan-ces, On my thumb he dan-ces,

         E    E     E  E    E    E     B    E
         E  F♯ G    G  G    B  C'B A   G F♯ E
         On my thumb thumb thumb, John-ny pup-pet dan-ces.
```

2 Little Johnny dances ⎱ repeat
   On my arm he dances ⎰
   On my arm, arm, arm,
   On my thumb, thumb, thumb,
   Johnny Puppet dances.

3 Little Johnny dances ⎱ repeat
   On my head he dances ⎰
   On my head . . . , arm . . . , thumb,
   Johnny Puppet dances.

You can go on making up verses for this song if you have older children. Start with one or two (at the most three) with little ones.

1 Let the children pretend they have a puppet by using one of their hands; they must act out all the verses and remember the sequence.

2 One day make a very simple puppet with the children and let them use it with their song.

string
card
toilet roll
newspaper

3 Invent a verse 'on the floor he dances'. Let the children make up a puppet dance. You can pretend you are holding the string. Every time you pull the string, the children must move a part of their body.

4 Try out the chime bar part with a child who can manage it.

5 When the tune is well known, clap the rhythm to

'Little Johnny dances' ♪♪♪♪ ♩ ♩

Ask the children what words (from the song) fit that rhythm. Then practise clapping it and whispering the words several times in succession. Play the same game another day. This time, ask one or two children to clap and whisper while you and everyone else sing the song. The next time give out instruments so that a small group can accompany the song.

6 When you have a helper try singing and acting the song with chimes and percussion.

7 Let the children paint pictures of puppets.

8 Make up a story using puppets.

London Bridge is Broken Down—
using notes F G A B♭ C' D'

Chimes

1 Lon-don Bridge is bro-ken down, bro-ken down, bro-ken down
Lon-don Bridge is bro-ken down, My fair la - dy.

2 Build it up with bricks and mortar, etc.
3 Bricks and mortar will not stay, etc.
4 Build it up with penny loaves, etc.
5 Penny loaves will mould away, etc.
6 Build it up with stones so strong, etc.
  Hurrah! 'twill last for ages long,
  My fair lady.

This is one of a number of versions of the song, and enables the children to act out one of their favourite games—building up and knocking down!

1 Use it as a singing game. Walk round in a circle on verses 1, 3, 5. Stand still and pretend to build on verses 2, 4, 6. Clap on the last two lines 'Hurrah!' etc.
2 Use it with percussion sitting in a group. Use different instruments on each verse, for example:
verse 1 Singing only
      2 Clappers
      3 Shakers
      4 Bells or tambourines
      5 Shakers
      6 All together

3 Combine percussion with the singing game. Let a few children play suitable instruments for the building actions on verses 2, 4 and 6.
4 Try out the chime bar part with a more able child of an older group.
5 When the children know the tune well, play a clapping game. You clap the rhythm for 'broken down' three times:

Ask the children which words from the song fit that rhythm ('London Bridge' fits:

but is not repeated twice more). Practise clapping this rhythm and whispering the words 'broken down' all together. Play the same game another day. This time ask one or two children to clap and whisper continuously while you all sing the song. The next time give out instruments so that a small group can accompany the song.
6 When you have a helper try singing the song with chimes and percussion.
7 Show the children a picture of London Bridge and, if you live near enough, visit it.
8 Make a big 'carton' model of London Bridge.
9 Make a scrapbook of bridges from pictures the children have brought and drawings they have made.
10 Another 'bridge' song is 'Sur le Pont d'Avignon'.

Sur le Pont d'Avignon—using notes C E F G A B♭ C'

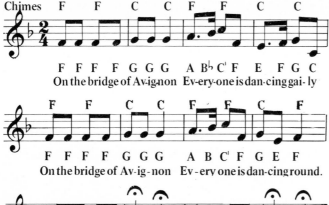

Chimes F   F   C   C   F   F   C   C

F F F   F G G   A B♭ C' F   E   F G C
On the bridge of Av-ig-non Ev-ery-one is dan-cing gai- ly

F   F   C   C   F   F   C   F

F F F   F G G   A B C' F   G E F
On the bridge of Av-ig-non Ev-ery one is dan-cing round.

F   FF   F G   F   F   F F G   F
Gen - tle-men go this way, La -dies go this   way.

(⌢ means pause on this note before continuing)

Sur le pont d'Avignon,
L'on y passe, l'on y danse,
Sur le pont d'Avignon,
L'on y danse tout en rond.

This is an old French nursery song and some children may know it in the original language! Older children may even prefer to sing it in French.

1   Use it as a singing game. Walk round in a circle to the 'dancing round' part. Act the verses and make up more verses of your own, such as:
Little boys go this way,
Little girls go this way.

Policemen go this way,
And policemen go that way, etc.

2   Add percussion to the chorus 'On the bridge . . . dancing round'. Let one or two children play tambourines the first time, then drums or clappers etc. They could sit in the middle of the circle, or stand outside.

3   Adapt this song for finger play when the children are sitting down. Make a bridge with fingers for 'On the bridge at Avignon'; let fingers dance for 'Everyone is dancing gaily' and repeat for the next two lines. If you have puppets let them act the verses for you; otherwise let the children mime as they sit.

4   Try out the chime bar part one day.

5   A good rhythm for percussion to accompany the song is

from the French words 'Sur le pont d'Avignon', or for older children

from the words 'Everyone is dancing gaily'. Introduce as a clapping game in the same way as the previous song 'London Bridge'.

6   When you have a helper try singing the song with chimes and percussion.

7   Talk to the children about France and about Avignon if you can. Show them a picture, if you have one, of what remains of the old bridge.

8   Link with the song 'London Bridge'.

38

Number One (*This Old Man*)—
using notes F G A B♭ C' D'

1   Number one, number one,
    Now my song has just begun,
    Tra-la . . . .
    Tra-la . . . .

2   Number two number two,
    I have learnt to tie my shoe,
    Tra-la, etc.

3   Number three . . .
    I can climb a great big tree, etc.

4   Number four . . .
    When you come in please shut the door, etc.

5   This little bee buzzes round his hive, etc.

6   We play drums with wooden sticks, etc.

7   Five and six will make eleven, etc.

8   See my dinner on my plate, etc.

9   See the bright stars twinkle and shine, etc.

10   We can start all over again, etc.

This is an all-purpose number song: you can alter
each rhyme to suit yourself.

1   Use it as a straightforward counting song. Have
cut-out wooden numbers, or number cards to hold up
for each verse: the children must hold up the right
number of fingers. Mime the second line and clap the
'tra-la' bit. Start with three verses with very small
children and gradually build it up.
2   Use it as a singing game. Count and mime on the
first two lines and walk (or skip) round in a circle to
'tra-la . . .'.
3   Sometimes when singing, leave out the last word of
the second line and hold up a picture as a cue. This is
good practice for aural identification of rhyming words.
With older children, hold up a flashcard of the actual
word as a cue.
4   Add percussion to the song on the 'tra-las'. Let
everyone play, or allocate specific instruments to each
verse.
5   Try the chime bar part with a more able child.
6   Sing the song with chimes and percussion when you
have your helper.
7   For more number songs the next section will be
helpful.

More about songs and rhymes

In many ways songs do a lot of incidental teaching for us, although this is not the main reason for singing with the children.

Singing together is fun. It can both stimulate and calm children; it offers valuable contact between us and the children and it provides controlled activity and movement—a blessing to all teachers in this changeable climate. Children learn to speak by imitation and repetition; they develop voice control through singing and body control through action songs; they begin to learn their numbers through counting songs and they learn to socialize through ring games and group activity.

A good working collection of these songs and rhymes is one of the most valuable teaching aids we can equip ourselves with. I have found it useful to make specific groupings as indicated in this section. You may prefer another method of prompting your memory.

Counting songs

Forwards
John Brown had a little motor car (three times)
One little motor car. Peep-peep!
John Brown had two motor cars
Two little motor cars. Peep-peep! Peep-peep! etc

One man went to mow, went to mow a meadow,
One man and his dog, went to mow a meadow,
Two men went to mow, went to mow a meadow,
Two men, one man and his dog went to mow a meadow.
etc

One little brown bird up and up he flew
Along came another one and that made two.
Two little brown birds sitting on a tree
Along came another one and that made three. etc

Number one, number one, now my song has just begun
With a nick nack paddy whack, give a dog a bone
This old man came rolling home.
Number two, number two, I have learnt to tie my shoe,
With a nick nack paddy whack etc

Peter works with one hammer, one hammer, one hammer,
Peter works with one hammer
All day long.
Peter works with two hammers etc

Backwards
Five little ducks went swimming one day
Over the pond and far away.
Mother Duck said, 'Quack, quack, quack',
But only four little ducks came back.
Four little ducks went swimming one day etc

Last verse:
One little duck went swimming one day
Over the pond and far away.
Mother Duck said 'Quack, quack, quack',
And five little ducks came swimming back.

Five little mice came out to play,
Gathering crumbs upon their way;
Out came a big fat pussy-cat—
And four little mice went scampering back.
(to the tune of *Five Little Ducks*)

Ten green bottles hanging on the wall,
Ten green bottles hanging on the wall,
And if one green bottle should accidentally fall,
There'd be nine green bottles hanging on the wall etc

Ten fat sausages sitting in the pan (twice)
One went 'pop' and another went 'bang'
There were eight fat sausages sitting in the pan etc
(to the tune of *Ten Green Bottles*)

40

Five currant buns in the baker's shop
Big and round with sugar on the top.
Along comes —— with a penny one day,
Gives it to the man, and takes one right away.

Four currant buns, etc.

No currant buns in the baker's shop
Big and round with sugar on the top,
Along comes Mummy (Mrs ——) with a penny one day
No currant buns so she goes right away.

Question and answer songs
Divide the group into half, or boys and girls, to sing
the question and answer; occasionally let a willing or
more able child sing the question or answer on his own.

Q Pussy cat, pussy cat, where have you been?
A I've been up to London to look at the Queen.
Q Pussy cat, pussy cat, what did you there?
A I frightened a little mouse under her chair. Miaow!

All Ding dong bell, pussy's in the well

Q Who put her in?
A Little Tommy Green.
Q Who pulled her out?
A Little Tommy Stout.

All What a naughty boy was that
     To harm poor pussy cat,
     Who ne'er did any harm
     But killed all the mice in his father's barn.

Q Mary, Mary quite contrary,
     How does your garden grow?
A With silver bells and cockle shells
     And pretty maids all in a row.

Q Do you know the Muffin man,
     The Muffin man, the Muffin man?
     Do you know the Muffin man
     Who lives in Drury Lane?
A Oh yes I (we) know the Muffin man etc

Q Polly put the kettle on (three times)
     We'll all have tea.
A Sukey take it off again (three times)
     They've all gone away.

Q Baa baa black sheep, have you any wool?
A Yes sir, yes sir, three bags full.

Q Little Boy Blue, come blow up your horn,
     The sheep's in the meadow, the cow's in the corn.
     Where's the boy that looks after the sheep?
A He's under the haycock fast asleep.
Q Will you wake him?
A No, not I,
     For if I do he'll be sure to cry.

Three little kittens they lost their mittens
And they began to cry;

Q 'Oh Mummy dear we greatly fear,
     Our mittens we have lost.'
A 'What, lost your mittens, you naughty kittens
     Then you shall have no pie!'
     Miaow! Miaow! Mew, mew, mew! (repeat)

Three little kittens they found their mittens,
And they began to cry;

Q 'Oh Mummy dear, look here, look here,
     Our mittens we have found!'
A 'What found your mittens, you good little kittens,
     Then you shall have some pie!'
     Miaow! Miaow! Mew, mew, mew! (repeat)

There's a hole in my bucket, dear Liza, dear Liza,
There's a hole in my bucket, dear Liza, in it.
Q With what shall I mend it? etc
A With a stone etc

Songs to help physical development
Chorus Here we go Lubin (Looby) Loo,
      Here we go Lubin (Looby) Light,
      Here we go Lubin (Looby) Loo,
      All on a Saturday night.

1 Put your right foot in,
  Put your right foot out,
  Shake it a little a little,
  And turn yourself about.
2 Put your left foot in etc
3 Put your right hand in etc
4 Put your left hand in etc
5 Put your head right in etc
6 Put your whole self in etc

We all clap hands together (three times)
And have a lovely time.
We all tap feet together etc
We all nod heads together etc

One finger, one thumb, keep moving (three times)
We all keep merry and bright.
One finger, one thumb, one arm keep moving etc

You put your right arm in, you put your right arm out,
You put your right arm in and you shake it all about,
You do the Hokey Cokey and you turn around,
And that's what it's all about.

Chorus Oh Hokey Cokey Cokey (three times)
       And that's what it's all about.

Using songs as a starter
Encourage the children to begin making up part of a song e.g.
Do you know the Muffin man etc
Do you know the
   The children can put in bus driver, soldier smart, milkman and so on. Some children will notice that there are three syllables to fill and say 'milkman tall' or the 'postman's son'.

Polly put the kettle on,
We'll all have tea.
Polly cut the bread up
Polly put the cakes out, etc.
Sukey take the cloth off
Sukey brush the crumbs up, etc.

   The children must try to fit their words to the tune: they will not be able to do this straight away and the extent to which they can suggest anything at all will depend upon their vocabulary and language development. It is important that you accept their ideas however ill-fitting they are at first and encourage more attempts.
   For the older and more able child, progress to songs like:

Thank you for waking me this morning,
Thank you for giving me today.
Thank you for every new day dawning
I'll be thanking you.

   It is essential that the tune is wellknown: the child can then try making up the last two lines beginning with 'Thank you . . .'.

Tunes for a special occasion
Sometimes it is difficult to find just the right song.
This is the time to try your own hand at song writing—
not the music, but the words. It is amazing how readily
tunes like *Mulberry Bush* and *Skip to my Lou*
accommodate new words.

1   Here we go round the apple tree (or the
    playground, or the birthday cake).

2   I'm as happy as can be,
    'Cause my mummy said to me,
    She's gonna take me to the nursery,
    Skip to my Lou my darlin'.

    I'll be glad when I get there,
    I'll take my doll and my Teddy Bear,
    If it rains, well I don't care!
    Skip to my Lou my darlin'.

    I know there'll be lots to do,
    Paints and toys and water too,
    If you come I'll play with you,
    Skip to my Lou my darlin'.

    I can't wait to start you see,
    Going to the nursery,
    I'll be happy as can be,
    Skip to my Lou my darlin'.

3   Oh dear what can the matter be,
    Oh dear what can the matter be,
    I don't like shopping on Saturday,
    Mummy, why can't we go home?
(to the tune of 'Oh dear what can the matter be?')

References
CARNIE, W. (1967) *Listening and Moving* London:
    Nelson
GRAY, V. and PERCIVAL, R. (1969) *Music Movement and
Mime for Children* London: Oxford University Press
MATTERSON, E. (1969) *This Little Puffin* Harmondsworth:
    Penguin
ROSS, D. (1966) *The Little Red Engine* series London:
    Faber and Faber
CHESTERMAN, L. (1935) *Music for the Nursery School*
    London: Harrap
SEEGER, R. (Ed.) (1948) *American Folk Songs for
    Children* New York: Doubleday
SANSOM, C. (no date) *Speech Rhymes* London: A. and
    C. Black
COBBY, M. and WARNER, I. M. (1961) *Listen to the
    Band* London: Pitman

4 Making simple percussion instruments

The joy of home-made instruments is that breakages don't matter; we can have as many as we feel we want to accommodate and we don't have to wait until the next financial year before we order. Many parents are pleased to make them in their own homes; big brothers and sisters love helping too. If you are part of a primary school or near to one, the junior teachers are often willing to make instruments as part of their craft work. Of course your own children will want to have a go and should be encouraged. But the bulk of your instruments will have to be sturdy and safe to handle and many of them, like the drums, cannot be successfully tackled by younger children. Try to get a good finish to each instrument, and remember that the children are attracted to the whole article—the look, the feel and the sound.

Shakers
You can use washing-up liquid containers, cosmetic bottles, tins, cardboard boxes or cylinders; virtually any container with rattly stuff inside constitutes a shaker. The important thing is to get as much variety in shape, material, size and sound as possible. Make sure that the lids are well secured by a strong glue otherwise the contents will be lost in no time.

I suggested in chapter 2 that you had a number of identical containers with different fillings, and a number of different containers with identical fillings. I suggested also that you try to use transparent containers for identification of the contents. Otherwise paint and decorate your shakers or cover them with *Contact*.

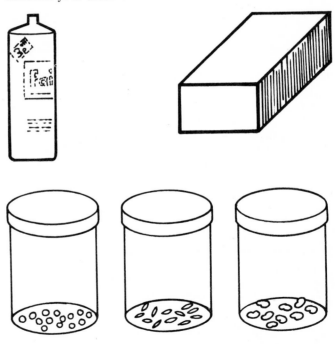

Maracca type shakers

Fill plastic lemons or shaped spice containers with rice or lentils, etc. Improvise handles from thin rods or newspaper; paint and varnish. Blow up a small balloon. Cover with a layer of damp tissue paper and then with about twelve layers of small bits of pasted newspaper (papier-mâché). Smooth down well and dry in between layers. When rock hard—in a few days' time—remove the balloon, fill with lentils (or rice) and glue in a handle from suitable sized dowelling. Paint and varnish.

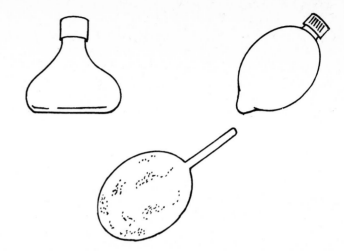

Clappers

For each pair of clappers you will need the base and lid of a wooden date box and two cotton reels. Sandpaper the wood and screw or stick the cotton reels onto the centre of the base and lid. Paint (two coats are best) and finish with a good clear varnish; this not only preserves the paint but improves the sound of the 'click'.

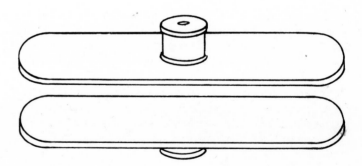

Coconuts—the authentic 'clip-clop'!
Smooth away the outside of a small coconut and get a
friend to help you saw it in half: it is a good idea to
pencil in the halfway mark. Scrape out the flesh and
when completely dry sandpaper all over. Bore a hole in
the centre of each half and improvise handles from
drawer-knobs or leather strips. Walnut-shell halves
make baby clip-clops!

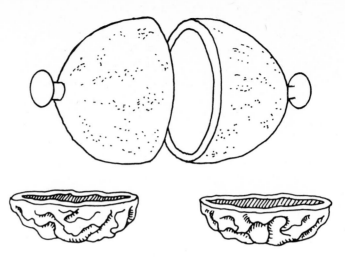

Rhythm-sticks
Get some dowelling from your local DIY shop. Choose
from 5mm and 15mm (or make two sizes) and cut into
lengths suitable for your children, say 150mm or 200mm
Sandpaper, especially the ends; paint and varnish in
bright colours.

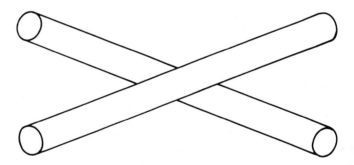

Bells

Use metal bottle tops (visit your local pub or off-licence), firm wire and a smooth piece of wood for the handle. Remove the plastic or cork lining of the bottle top if there is one and make a hole in the centre by hammering a nail through onto a piece of old wood. Thread onto the wire and secure each end into the wooden handle which can be painted and varnished.

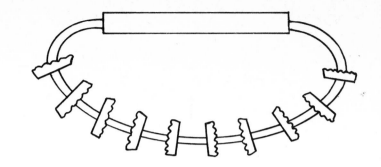

Jingles

These are made from metal bottle tops, and a longish piece of wood, about 150 x 35 x 10mm. Drive a nail through the bottle tops and into the wood, putting at least two bottle tops onto each nail. Paint and varnish.

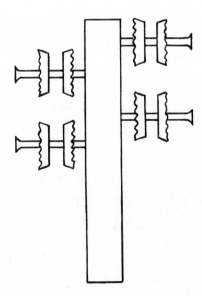

Tambourines

Three paper picnic plates glued firmly together form the basis of the tambourine. The children themselves can paint both sides; then put on preferably two coats of varnish—this helps durability as well as tone. Punch holes about 15mm from the edge all round. Thread two metal bottle tops onto an open curtain ring or firm wire and fasten through the holes. Arrange the bottle tops back-to-back to get a brighter sound. You could use small bells or anything else that jingles. Finish off by threading gaily coloured ribbons through alternate holes, or otherwise fasten jingles all round.

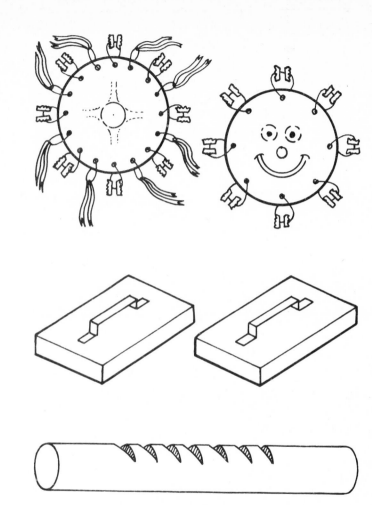

Sand blocks

Cover the ends of two blocks of wood of handling size with sandpaper using glue or drawing pins. Improvise handles if necessary.

Scrapers (Guiros)

Saw notches across a piece of bamboo and use a rhythm stick or something similar for scraping. Reeded hardboard, or a wooden washboard also make good scrapers.

Triangles

A suspended horseshoe, or smooth piece of metal hit with a large nail sounds good. Supervise closely.

Drums

Drums are firm favourites with most children and what a godsend the rubber type are! When well made they produce a handsome sound and one that is tolerable even at its loudest and fiercest.

The best material is a piece of rubber from an old inner tube from a car or lorry tyre, so make friends with a local garage or tyre repair shop. One snag is that inner tubes are often made from synthetic rubber. This is difficult to handle and produces a 'dead' sound. So check carefully: the reddish coloured tube is usually reliable and of good rubber.

Next the tin—a cylindrical biscuit, coffee or cake tin will do—cadge one from a local shop. Just remove the lid and paint or cover the tin with *Contact*. Cut a circular piece of rubber, allowing an overlap of about 50mm, and punch holes about 25mm from the outer edge: reinforce at the back with cloth washers.

Thread round the edge with twine, thick string or long football- or shoe-laces. Place over the top of the tin, pull tight and secure. Now lace the top onto the tin with the help of a curtain ring under the bottom, twine and, if possible, a helper. This bit requires firm handling and patience. When tightening the tension, pull the rubber itself and not the string, as this sometimes splits the holes.

A double-headed drum can be made from a stronger tin like a paint or whitewash tin. Remove both the lid and the base of the tin, making sure that there are no sharp edges left. Use two circles of rubber and lace in the same way.

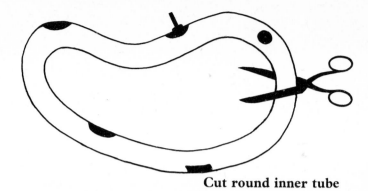

Cut round inner tube

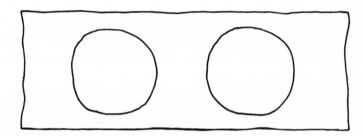

Open out tube and cut out two circles

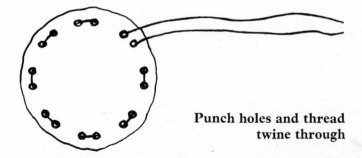

Punch holes and thread twine through

50

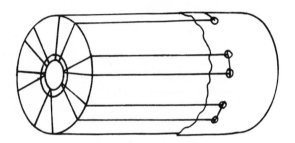

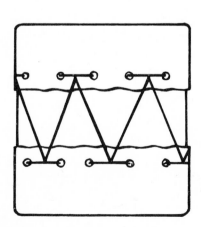

Drumsticks

Make a hole in a solid hardwood ball and glue in a piece of dowel rod.

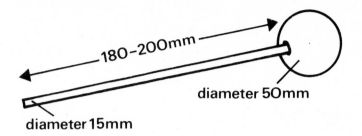

180–200mm

diameter 50mm

diameter 15mm

Pitched instruments

Stretch elastic bands of different thicknesses over a lidless cigar box or something similar.

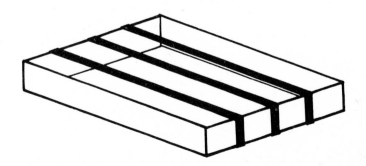

Cigar boxes can also make *tone-blocks*. Cut shapes out of the lid or sides, then glue or nail the lid on. Hit with a rhythm or drum stick.

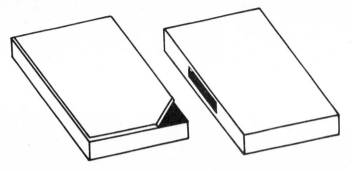

If you are interested enough to want to go on to make a simple xylophone from wood, chimes from brass or copper tubing, or a glockenspiel from aluminium alloy, then I suggest that you refer to one of the books mentioned below.

References

BLOCKSIDGE, K. (1974) *Making Musical Instruments* London: Nursery School Association of Great Britain and Northern Ireland

MANDEL, M. and WOOD, R. (1970) *Make Your Own Musical Instruments* Folkestone: Bailey

ROBERTS, R. (1965) *Musical Instruments made to be Played* Leicester: Dryad Press

WILLIAMS, P. (1971) *Lively Craft Cards* London: Mills and Boon

5 Audio-visual aids for the teacher

A skilled teacher can obtain a good deal of help from the radio, the record player and the tape recorder. She can use them to provide music for the children to move to; for songs and games; as a means of encouraging listening, and as a valuable source of teaching ideas.

Although we would all agree that young children should get their experience of musical sound at first hand, few of us can provide in live form an adequate range of musical experiences. Most children are exposed to music at home, through the radio, television and records, and if we decide to use any of these media in the classroom, it is important that we encourage good attitudes and listening habits that will also benefit the young home listener.

Ideas for using radio
There are suitable programmes on the main channels (e.g. *Listen with Mother*), on local radio stations (e.g. *Pattercake* on Radio London) and on the School Broadcasting network (e.g. *Music and Movement*, *Playtime*, *A Corner for Music* and *Music Box*); then there is a wealth of music from pop to classical put out throughout the day that can be used for clapping, dancing, moving or listening.

Find out from the *Radio Times* what is available and suitable. Write for an up-to-date coverage of school programmes to: The School Broadcasting Council for the United Kingdom, The Langham, Portland Place, London W1. Then select the programme(s) you want and get the teachers' notes (school radio) which can be purchased from: BBC Publications, 35 Marylebone High Street, London W1. If you do all this well before you start using the programme, you will get a better idea of whether it is really suitable.

It is worthwhile considering taping the programme as the broadcast timing is often unsuitable, and the whole idea is to use these programmes at the *right* time for *you*. There are many other advantages to be gained from recording programmes (technical advice about the recording process is given at the end of this chapter):

1   You can hear the recording in advance
2   The recording is available to more than one group of children
3   You can stop the programme to rehear bits or to enlarge on or explain them if necessary
4   You can hear it again another day
5   You can keep especially good programmes, or store a whole series that you find successful
6   Programmes like *Music and Movement* progress during the year. You may find the September-October programmes more suitable for your children. You can

then use these throughout the year. Label the cassette or spool tape clearly and in adequate detail to facilitate quick identification

7 You are completely free to timetable your own day
8 You may find that although you decide not to use the programme, you will get ideas that will extend your own teaching.

Using records

There is much valuable recorded material in the form of songs, singing games, listening music, music to move to and illustrated stories. Go to your local record shop or browse in the record department of your public library (if there is one). Write to the main record companies for their catalogues or lists of children's records (see also Appendix 4).

Problems do arise in the use of the record in the classroom: we probably only want to use part of one side, and if this bit is in the middle, finding the right place may be tricky with a room full of children. Then the needle often jumps if the children are dancing to the record; and I haven't mentioned the chore of getting the turntable and record. . . . These problems vanish if you have learnt to put the material you want to use on tape. This is not difficult, and a skill that is worthwhile acquiring: read through the notes at the end of this chapter.

Try taping short excerpts from the children's favourite records (or your own!). Choose contrasted sequences, e.g.:

Dance of the Mirlitons (or Reed-pipes) from *The Nutcracker Suite* by Tchaikovsky—light
March from *The Love of Three Oranges* by Prokofiev—march

Peter's Tune from *Peter and the Wolf* by Prokofiev—gay
In the Hall of the Mountain King from *Peer Gynt* by Grieg—dramatic
The Swan from *Carnival of the Animals* by Saint-Saëns—quiet, lyrical

Label the tape in sufficient detail and keep it accessible. You can use this kind of tape in many ways. Let the children clap and move to it. Use it with an informal percussion group. When you need a short piece of 'settling' music, perhaps at the end of the morning, select a suitable item like 'The Swan'. You may be singing a soldier song and want some more soldier music; use the 'March' or something similar if you have recorded it. I am sure you will find that the time involved in making this kind of tape will be well spent.

Further uses for the tape recorder

I found that making my own tapes gave me a much more flexible approach to some aspects of music making, especially percussion, for I became completely independent of the piano, and therefore of the use of the hall. I was also able to listen and play *with* the children. One of the tapes consisted of simple tunes that the children knew, played on a variety of instruments (by myself) and programmed so that each piece contrasted in some way with the next one, and was preceded by a short 'thinking' signal:

(piano) *The Grand Old Duke of York*—march
(piano) *Boys and girls come out to play*—skipping
(xylophone) *Yankee Doodle*—running
(glockenspiel) *Twinkle, twinkle little star*—quietly

(piano) *London Bridge is broken down*—heavy
(glockenspiel) *As I lay on the golden sands*—light, swaying
(piano) *Baa, baa black sheep*—steady, march

I use this tape for clapping, singing, percussion, moving and listening. Similar tapes can be made without using the piano, if you cannot play and do not know a cooperative friend or parent who is also a pianist. Use the chimes, borrow a xylophone and sing some of the songs.

It takes time, good judgment and care making tapes, but in my opinion the effort is well worth it. Once made, the tapes are always available and you can go on adding to them. Remember to label each tape clearly and keep them handy. Here are some more ideas:

1   Make up a puzzle tape of everyday sounds—tap running, footsteps, dog barking, baby crying, aeroplane overhead, door shutting, kettle whistling, spoon in a teacup.

2   Make up a puzzle tape of radio and TV jingles and programme music, e.g. *The Wombles, Playschool* signature tune, *Jackanory, Blue Peter, Magic Roundabout*, etc.

3   Record some favourite nursery rhymes, fingerplay songs and current children's songs. Sing them yourself or get a friend to help you. This tape can be used by the children who like to tuck themselves away in a quiet corner.

With the children:
1   Let the children suggest sounds to record. Play back to another group as a quiz.

2   Let the children record their own little stories. At first they will be a bit rambling or just what comes into their mind. When they have become more skilful write the stories down in a book and let the children illustrate them. Later on the older or more able children can try recording their stories with sound effects!

Technical help

Choosing a tape recorder
There are four types of machine: reel-to-reel recorder; cassette recorder; cassette player; combined radio and cassette recorder.

Reel-to-reel recorder
You put a reel (spool) of tape on one spindle, and attach the tape to an empty reel on a second spindle after threading it through a central mechanism. Advantages—the sound quality can be very good, most of the machines give plenty of volume, and you can edit the tape. Disadvantages—threading the tape can be rather fiddly, and the machines tend to be big and heavy.

Cassette recorder
You simply snap in a cassette and switch on. Advantages—machines are very easy to operate, light in weight and can be quite cheap. Disadvantages—unless you pay a lot of money the sound quality and loudness are not up to reel-to-reel standards; editing is difficult. Some cassette recorders work on batteries, but these run down fairly quickly and it is probably cheaper in the long run to buy a battery/mains machine.

Cassette player
This plays cassettes that have already been made on a cassette recorder. Advantages: cheap, very portable, easily operated even by a young child, and tapes cannot be erased by mistake. If you can afford to do so, buy a cassette recorder which you keep at home to make your recordings, and one or two players for use with, or by, the children.

Combined radio and cassette recorder
With this, recording a radio broadcast simply involves pressing a couple of buttons.

To get advice on the actual model to meet your needs, consult the audio-visual adviser if your education department employs one. If not, a free advisory service is available from the National Audio Visual Aids Centre, Belsize Road, London NW6. Advice is also available from the Scottish Centre for Educational Technology, 131A Renfrew Street, Glasgow WC3.

All machines need regular maintenance. It is especially important to clean the 'head' periodically. This isn't difficult if you follow the instruction book.

Making recordings

Using a microphone
It is best to use the microphone supplied with the machine. Read the instruction book carefully, especially with regard to the recording level. If the recorder has a manual/automatic level switch, you will get better results on the manual setting as long as you follow the instructions. Experiment with the distance between the microphone and whatever you are recording in order to get crisp quality and to minimize echoes. Remember that the quality can be affected by the size and furnishing of the room and, if possible, try different

rooms. Don't embark on a long and difficult recording without first making a short trial and checking the result. Take trouble over the details and you will get surprisingly good results from even the cheapest equipment.

From record player or radio
If you put the microphone in front of the loudspeaker the result will be poor. Most record players and radios have an output socket which can be connected by a special lead to the tape recorder. This is the way to get really good quality. Your audio-visual adviser can probably help you: otherwise, consult a local dealer. With a little care, you can make a recording that sounds almost as good as the original.

Getting technical assistance
If there is a local audio-visual adviser, he will be glad to help you. Otherwise it is quite likely that a parent of one of your children is something of a technical expert, and can show you how to fix things up. And the local radio dealer will probably be helpful if you tell him who you are. Modern equipment can be so good that there is really no excuse for subjecting children to poor quality sound.

Copyright
In certain circumstances copying from radio or gramophone records is subject to the copyright law. The BBC have made a special arrangement that permits the copying of school broadcasts.

6 Basic musical knowledge for the teacher

Although it is not necessary to be able to read music in order to develop musical activities with your children, some knowledge is useful especially when you would like to know what a new song sounds like. There may be a friend or member of staff who can sing it through for you, otherwise you are stuck unless you can read the melody line. This in itself is not difficult if you have chime bars, a small glockenspiel or a piano to work with.

It is possible to make tuned instruments as in chapter 4, but the sound must be accurate: toy instruments are not suitable. Unless you are handy at this kind of thing I would strongly advise you to invest in either a small glockenspiel or a set of chime bars—depending upon how much you can afford. The smallest suitable glockenspiel will cost about £4.50: chime bars are about £1 each, and the following range of notes recommended for tune making will cost approximately £12; C D E F G A B C' D' E' and F♯ and B♭. However, these can be bought singly or a few at a time according to available funds. The advantage of chime bars is that they can be used separately or in small groups of two or three, and are, from my experience, easier for small children to play.

The following section is presented as a brief introduction to reading children's songs. Read it

through, but don't worry about memorizing or learning facts. Use it as a reference when you are trying out a new song.

Signs and accent

The signs we use to represent *sounds* are called *notes*; those for *silences* are called *rests*. This table shows the relative values or lengths of notes and rests:

Musical term	*Sign*	*Equivalent rest*
Semi-breve (whole)	𝅝	▬
Minims (halves)	𝅗𝅥 𝅗𝅥	▬
Crotchets (quarters)	𝅘𝅥 𝅘𝅥 𝅘𝅥 𝅘𝅥	𝄽
Quavers (eighths)	𝅘𝅥𝅮𝅘𝅥𝅮 𝅘𝅥𝅮𝅘𝅥𝅮 𝅘𝅥𝅮𝅘𝅥𝅮 𝅘𝅥𝅮𝅘𝅥𝅮	𝄾
Semi-quavers (sixteenths)	𝅘𝅥𝅯𝅘𝅥𝅯𝅘𝅥𝅯𝅘𝅥𝅯 𝅘𝅥𝅯𝅘𝅥𝅯𝅘𝅥𝅯𝅘𝅥𝅯 𝅘𝅥𝅯𝅘𝅥𝅯𝅘𝅥𝅯𝅘𝅥𝅯 𝅘𝅥𝅯𝅘𝅥𝅯𝅘𝅥𝅯𝅘𝅥𝅯	𝄿

Any one of these notes may be followed by a dot which increases the value of the note by half its original value:

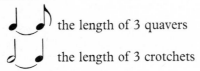

♩ 1 minim   = 2 crotchets

♩. 1½ minims = 3 crotchets

♩ 1 crotchet = 2 quavers

♩. 1½ crotchets = 3 quavers

A note may also be lengthened by being 'tied' to another note:

the length of 3 quavers

the length of 3 crotchets

Accent

In speech we lay stress on certain words. Similarly in music we stress or accent certain notes and this accent usually occurs at regular intervals. In order to indicate the recurring strong beat a sign called a *bar line* is used: this divides the notes into bars with the strong beat coming immediately after the bar line, thus:

1   2   3   4   1   2   3   4
Baa   baa   black sheep, Have you a - ny wool?

1   2   3   4   1   2   3   4
Yes   sir,   yes   sir, Three bags full.

Time and rhythm

This is an important ingredient of the character of a tune—the way it moves, and whether it is a march, a waltz or a skipping kind of tune.

Music moves along in regular beats which are usually grouped in 2s, 3s or 4s, for example:

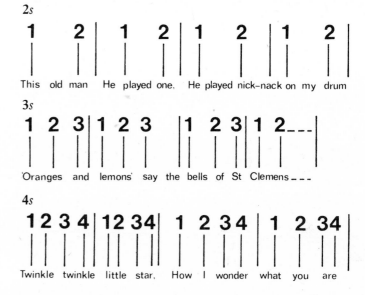

2s

1   2 | 1   2 | 1   2 | 1   2

This old man He played one. He played nick-nack on my drum

3s

1 2 3 | 1 2 3 | 1 2 3 | 1 2 _ _ _

'Oranges and lemons' say the bells of St Clemens _ _ _

4s

1 2 3 4 | 1 2 3 4 | 1 2 3 4 | 1 2 3 4

Twinkle twinkle little star. How I wonder what you are

This information, called a *time signature* is given at the beginning of every piece of music just after the clef:

(The clef fixes the exact position of the notes in the treble or bass.)

58

It can be written in any of the following ways:

The top figure denotes the *number* of beats in a bar and the bottom figure the *kind* of beat (halves, quarters, eighths etc).

These three examples all have 4 at the bottom, indicating a crotchet, or ¼ beat—most frequently used in children's songs:

This is known as *simple time* as the beat is divisible by two.

The other kind of music frequently found in children's songs and games is the *skipping* or *lilting* kind: this is shown by a ⁶⁄₈ time signature which means 6 quavers (eights) in a bar, for example:

usually written

a quaver has half the length of a crotchet.

This is called *compound time* because the beat is divisible by three. 'Oh dear what can the matter be?' is a good example:

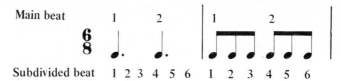

The *skipping rhythm* looks like this:

More about dotted notes
The dot lengthens the time of a note by half its original value. The first note in this rhythm is lengthened and the second note shortened, giving the tune a little jerk as in:

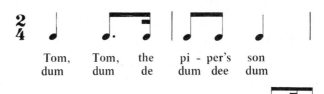

Tom, Tom, the pi - per's son
dum dum de dum dee dum

Observe the same effect of the rhythm in *Ride-a-cock horse*:

Ride a cockhorse to Ban - bu - ry Cross to
dum de dee dum dee dum de dee dum dee

Melody

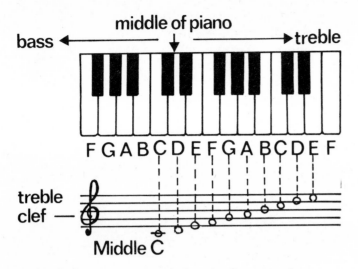

Musical notes are named after the first seven letters of the alphabet A—G and they follow that order. Getting to know the notes on a piano keyboard is quite easy if you first of all observe the pattern of the black keys: these are arranged in alternate bunches of twos and threes and enable you to spot the right white key for any note almost automatically. For instance, if you are looking for a C, observe that it is always the white key just in front of a group of two black ones. Note D is the white key lying between two black ones. The keys for notes E F and B C have no black keys in between. Chime bars have their note names written on them; just arrange them in the right order following the arrangement of the piano keyboard illustrated above.

The black keys produce a sound that is halfway in pitch between the two white keys they lie between. For instance, the black key between the white keys for notes F and G produces a sound a little above (sharper) than F or a little below (flatter) than G. Hence it can be called F sharp, written:

or G flat, written:

Musical notes are written down on a staff which originally consisted of a series of eleven lines: this is now divided into two sections of five lines each—the upper five representing the notes above middle C and the lower five those below middle C. The treble clef (French for 'key') identifies the upper staff which covers the melodic range of children's songs. All the lines and spaces are used.

The keynote

The music of all children's songs (and most western music) is centred round one principal note called the *keynote* or 'home' note, and is said to be in the key of that note. The notes lying between any keynote and its octave (8 notes) above or below, when arranged in a particular pattern are called a *Scale* (scala—a ladder). Here are the notes of three of the most common keys:

Key C using notes C D E F G A B C
Key G using notes G A B C D E F♯ G
Key F using notes F G A B♭ C D E F

Play these three scales on a piano, glockenspiel or

chime bars and try to 'hear' the reason why the black keys are used in the scales of G and F. You should hear the same sound pattern as that produced by the notes of scale C. The key signature at the beginning of a piece of music indicates the key in which the music is written:

is in Key C using no black keys

is in Key G with F♯ instead of F

is in Key F with B♭ instead of B

The range of chime bars recommended—C D E F G A B C' D' E' and F♯ and B♭ will enable you to play tunes in these three keys.

When working out a new tune:

1 note the time signature—$\frac{2}{4}$ $\frac{3}{4}$ $\frac{4}{4}$ or $\frac{6}{8}$
2 note the key signature
3 clap the rhythm of the notes

4 work out the melody
5 play through and sing
6 get some practise by playing some songs that you already know. Try out the notated tunes at the back of this book.

I have given you a skeleton introduction to musical theory. If you want to learn more by yourself try Howard Shanet's practical book *Learn to Read Music*.

Using the piano

Many pianos stand idle because there is no one who can play a Chopin waltz or a Beethoven slow movement. This is a pity because the piano is a versatile instrument, and whilst it is an advantage to be able to play it well, the non-pianist should not discard it altogether. Many players unfortunately misuse the piano as a teaching aid. Playing to young children should be very simple and clear; it is better to play a melody for instance in the right hand only, rather than back it up with thick chords, blurred by the continuous use of the 'loud' pedal. It could be a distinct advantage to the children if you were only able to use one hand at a time. If you have the use of a piano, I suggest you explore it—discover the kind of sound you can get from the various parts of the keyboard: try little runs on two or three notes in the treble (right hand end); try some heavy notes, several heavy notes in the bass (left hand end); try playing a bunched-up group of notes quietly in the middle of the piano. Try different ideas all over the piano. Experiment with the right, or sustaining, pedal (it does just that—sustains the sound until you remove your foot).

Once you are a little more confident, try some of the ideas on the following pages.

Piano keyboard

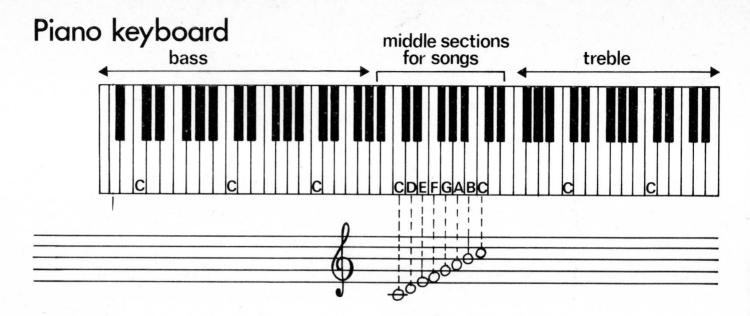

bass   middle sections for songs   treble

Giants—in the bass
1   Big steps—heavy ponderous loud notes—anywhere. Use both hands. Clashing notes don't matter. Soft playing for a giant creeping.
2   Roar or anger—trill two notes in the bass continuously. Use the pedal. Use two hands if you can.
3   Climbing—slow loud notes from one C to the next and down again.
4   Sleeping—soft chords consisting of two notes a third (three notes) apart like CE or EG. Gently press them down together.

Fairies or *birds*—in the treble
1   Running or tripping—play two adjacent notes lightly and continuously in succession, say CD or FG in a running style. Change to another two notes. Keep

changing. Try using two hands. Keep the effect light. Don't worry about clashes of sound.
2   Skipping (fairies)—play two adjacent notes in a skipping rhythm, e.g.:

C   CD   DC   CD   D G   GF   FG   GF   F

3   Flying up—play lightly up from C to C either as a scale or like this:
CDE, DEF, EFG, FGA, GAB, ABC
4   Flying down—play down in the same way.
5   Sleeping—soft chords as for giants.

Rabbits or *grasshoppers*—anywhere in the middle or treble sections
1 Hopping—play two notes, a fifth (5 notes) apart, in quick succession in a downward direction: emphasize (>) the second note, e.g.

GC GC CF CF GC GC
 >   >   >   >   >   >

Use two sets of notes, as above, to begin with; then play anywhere as you become more experienced.
2 Twiddle whiskers or nose (rabbits)—trill two adjacent notes continuously.

Wriggly worms—in the middle section
Slide down a few notes with the back part of your thumb using the nail. Do this gently in different parts of this section of the keyboard. Occasionally trill two adjacent notes.

Cats—in the middle section
1 Stalking—light, fairly stealthy notes anywhere in this section, but keep the notes within a limited range, say an octave (8 notes).
2 Springing—literally spring from one note to another—say from C to G, from F to C in an upward direction. Spring down in the same way for a downward jump.
3 Miaow—play four or five successive notes like this:

Mi — aou
 G   F E D C

Dogs—in the middle section
1 Running—play two adjacent notes in quick succession in a running style. Change to another pair of notes to get variety.
2 Barking—strike two notes a fifth (5 notes) apart sharply together, e.g. C G.

Weather
1 Thunder—a rumble in the bass.
2 Lightning—a sharp slide with the thumb nail in the treble.
3 Raindrops—light notes played quickly in the treble, or little downward runs—EDC, GFE, FED, anywhere. Keep to the treble.
4 Heavy rain—trill two adjacent notes continuously in the middle section. Use two hands to make the sound 'heavier'.
5 Hail—short sharp notes in the middle section.
6 Sunshine—play some notes gently one after the other, using the sustaining (right) pedal, in the middle or treble sections. Keep within the compass of an octave (8 notes).

Soldiers—in the middle and bass sections
The basis for a march is a steady beat in 4 time, e.g.

or

63

Use three notes C E G in the middle section. Play firmly using your thumb (on C) middle finger (on E) and little finger (on G) of your *right hand*. Start and finish on C, the key or 'home' note. Work out a tune, e.g.

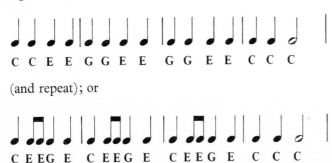

C C E E G G E E   G G E E C C C

(and repeat); or

C EEG E   C EEG E   C EEG E   C C C

If you can use your *left hand* as well, play the same notes C E G lower down in the bass. Try these ideas:

1 use the same tune as the right hand
2 play at half the speed using C all the time
3 play at half the speed using C and G all the time
4 design your own left hand accompaniment on these three notes.

Rhythm

R.H.   C   C   E   E   G G E E   G G E   E   C C C

L.H. (8 notes lower) or											
1C	C	E	E	G	G	E	E	G	G	E	E C C C
or 2 C		C		C		C		C		C		C C
or 3 C		G		C		G		C		G		C C

Make up more marching tunes in 4 time using these sets of notes:

F A C—with F as the key note
G B D—with G as the key note

Running tunes—in the middle **and** treble sections
These tunes are usually in 2 time with a running or quaver rhythm like *Bobby Shaftoe* or *Yankee Doodle*. Use the same notes as for the march—C E G—and play lightly in a running style with your *right hand*:

C C E E G G E E   G G E E C C C

If you can use your left hand play the same notes an octave (8 notes) lower.

Then try the same ideas as suggested for the march, but keep your left hand very light:

Rhythm

R.H.   C C E E   G G E E   G G E E   C C C

L.H. (8 notes lower) or								
1C C E E	G G E E	G G E E	C C C
or 2 C C	C C	C C	C C
or 3 C G	C G	C G	C C

4 Design your own left hand accompaniment on C A G. Make up more running tunes in 2 time using F A C and G B D.

Skipping tunes—in the middle and treble sections
Use the same rhythm as *Boys and Girls come out to play* or *Humpty Dumpty*:

skip   and skip   and   skip   and skip   and

Adapt ideas from the running and marching suggestions:

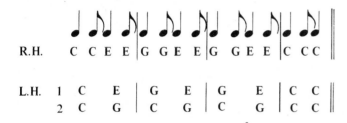

R.H.   C   C E E | G   G E   E | G   G E E | C   C C ‖

L.H.   1   C   E | G   E | G   E | C   C ‖
       2   C   G | C   G | C   G | C   C ‖

Continue with notes F A C and G B D. Experiment with your own ideas.

Galloping tunes—in the middle and bass sections
Use a $\frac{6}{8}$ time with a dotted note to give a little jerk, e.g.

gal - lop and gal - lop and   gal - lop and gal - lop and

This is a fairly fast rhythm and needs practice. I suggest you start like this:

play 4 times

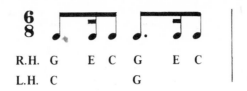

R.H. G   E   C   G   E   C
L.H. C   G

change to and play 4 times

C   A   F   C   A   F
F   C

Keep repeating. Then experiment with your own ideas.

Very few little children can skip and gallop, so introduce these movements with discretion. Saying the words rhythmically helps. Let the children listen to you clapping or playing the rhythm and let them join in clapping.

Once you have mastered the art of tune making on three notes, begin to use the five notes that lie within the compass of the hand, e.g.

C	D	E	F	G
thumb	first	second	third	fourth	fingers

G	A	B	C	D

(F   G   A   B♭   C)

E

Then progress on to a marching tune:

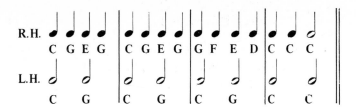

a running tune:

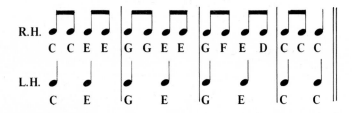

a skipping tune:

Movement through nursery rhymes

Marching
Aitken Drum
London Bridge
Grand Old Duke of York
Old King Cole

Walking
Hot cross buns
Peas Pudding Hot
Baa Baa Black Sheep
Frère Jacques
Ring-a-ring of roses

Tiptoe
Twinkle, twinkle little star
Lavender's blue

Quietly
Mary, Mary quite contrary
Little Bo-Peep

Running
I had a little nut tree
Bobby Shaftoe
Yankee Doodle
Polly put the kettle on
Lucy Locket

Skipping
Boys and girls come out to play
Humpty Dumpty
Jack and Jill
Mulberry Bush

Galloping
Ride a cock horse
Pat-a-cake

Hopping
Tom, Tom, the piper's son

Bouncing
Humpty Dumpty
Hey diddle diddle

Swaying
Pussy cat, pussy cat
See-saw Margery Daw
Rock a bye baby
I love little pussy
Oh where and oh where has my little dog gone

Some tunes are 'all-purpose'. Vary the speed and they will fit practically any movement:

Aitken Drum
Mulberry Bush
Boys and girls come out to play
Jack and Jill

A list of recommended books is given at the end of this chapter.

Hearing a sound
What is happening when you 'hear a chime bar'? Tapping the bar causes it to vibrate at a steady rate (you can feel the movement if you touch it lightly with a fingertip). The vibrations are picked up by the air in contact with the bar. Then they spread out in all

directions through the air surrounding the bar until they reach your eardrums, which vibrate at the same rate. This causes a message to pass to your brain which tells you that it hears a sound corresponding to that rate of vibration.

The sound travels through the air at a speed of about one mile every five seconds. (Watch someone hammering in the distance and notice that you see each stroke *before* you hear it because light travels much faster than sound.)

Anything that vibrates at a suitable rate produces sound. It can be the diaphragm of a drum which, like a chime bar, is set vibrating by tapping; the string of a violin, set vibrating by bowing; the air inside a recorder, which vibrates when you blow into the mouthpiece; or a loudspeaker, which is made to vibrate by electric current.

Sound travels through liquids (try an experiment in the bath) and solid materials, as well as through air and other gases.

Loudness
As you might expect, the bigger the vibrations, the louder the sound. Children discover this only too easily.

Pitch
The pitch of a note is determined by the rate of vibration, or the 'frequency'. Thus middle A—the note on which orchestras tune up—corresponds to a frequency of 440 vibrations per second. The lowest note on a piano has a frequency of about 25 vibrations per second and the highest note about 3500. A percussive sound (drum, cymbals) doesn't seem to have a definite pitch because it is made up of a jumble of frequencies.

It is worth knowing, in order to understand

descriptions of sound apparatus, that the technical way of saying so many 'vibrations per second' is so many 'cycles per second' or so many 'Hertz' (often abbreviated to 'Hz').

Overtones
When a note is played on a musical instrument, higher notes are also automatically produced, which have frequencies double, treble, etc. the note played. Thus, when you play middle A (440 Hz) you also produce notes with frequencies 880 Hz, 1760 Hz and so on. These higher notes are called overtones. You may be able to hear the first overtone if you listen carefully.

Quality
The same note has a different quality when played on different types of instruments. This is because the relative strengths of the overtones vary with the instrument. A tuning fork does not produce overtones; hence its 'pure' sound. A 'rich' sound is made up of many frequencies. Very high notes seem thin because the overtones are beyond our limit of hearing.

Limit of hearing
The highest frequency that we can hear decreases as we get older. An adult may not be able to hear frequencies above 12000 Hz, but a young child's hearing may go up to 16000 Hz or higher. This has an important implication for the selection of radio, record player and tape recorder. The sibilants and explosives of speech (s, p, t, f etc) contain very high frequencies which may not be properly reproduced by poor equipment. Unfortunately the intelligibility of speech depends on them, and young children not yet secure with language may therefore have difficulty in understanding speech from equipment that has

inadequate high frequency performance. So listen critically to apparatus before you accept it and, if in doubt, get children to help you. Some guide to comparative performance can be obtained from manufacturers' brochures, which usually specify the upper frequency limit. And when using equipment with a tone control, check that it is set to give plenty of treble: if it is turned down, the higher frequencies are not reproduced.

References
BERRY, M. and DINN, F. (1953) *Sing Dance and Play* London: Schott and Company
BUCK, P. (1961) *The Oxford Nursery Song Book* London: Oxford University Press
HUDSON, H. (1972) *Nursery Rhymes with a New Look* London: Edwin Ashdown
JOHNSON, M. B. (1951) *One-a-week* London: J. Curwen and Sons
SHANET, H. (1969) *Learn to Read Music* London: Faber and Faber

Appendix 1 Sources of songs and rhymes

Down by the station *This Little Puffin* Harmondsworth: Penguin

Five currant buns in the baker's shop *This Little Puffin* Harmondsworth: Penguin

Five little ducks went swimming one day *This Little Puffin* Harmondsworth: Penguin

Five little mice came out to play *This Little Puffin* Harmondsworth: Penguin

Here comes a big red bus *This Little Puffin* Harmondsworth: Penguin

Here comes a policeman riding on a bicycle *Echo and Refrain Songs* London: Stainer and Bell

High and low, Fast and slow *Speech Rhymes* London: A. and C. Black

John Brown had a little motor-car (adapted from John Brown had a little Indian) *This Little Puffin* Harmondsworth: Penguin

Little Johnny Puppet *Anthologie des Chants Populaires Français* Paris: Durand et Cie

My motor is humming *Speech Rhymes* London: A. and C. Black

One little brown bird up and up he flew *The Oxford School Music Books—Infant Book* London: Oxford University Press

Peter works with one hammer *This Little Puffin* Harmondsworth: Penguin

Pitter-patter, pitter-patter *Speech Rhymes* London: A. and C. Black

Pray open your umbrella *Fingers and Thumbs* London: Stainer and Bell

Puffer train, puffer train *Music for the Infant School* London: Harrap

Rain on the house-top *Speech Rhymes* London: A. and C. Black

Ring the bell! *Speech Rhymes* London: A. and C. Black

Summer goodbye *Sixty Songs for Little Children* London: Oxford University Press

Ten fat sausages sitting in the pan *This Little Puffin*
   Harmondsworth: Penguin

Thank you for giving me this morning *Faith, Folk and
   Clarity* Norfolk: Galliard

The music makers *Listen to the Band* London: Pitman

The wheels on the bus go round and round *This Little
   Puffin* Harmondsworth: Penguin

When you beat on the drum *Thirty Folk Settings for
   Children* London: Curwen

Appendix 2 Song books for nursery and reception classes

There are very many children's song books published. Here is a list of those I have worked with; as a guide I have asterisked the ones I have found most helpful with very young children. For a fuller list write to: The British Association for Early Childhood Education, Montgomery Hall, The Oval, Kennington, London SE11 5SW

Children's Singing Games (*Set 1* and *11*) by Gomme and Sharp, London: Novello

Clarendon Book of Carols and Songs by Wiseman and Northcote, London: Oxford University Press

Echo and Refrain Songs by Elizabeth Barnard, London: Stainer and Bell

Eight Singing Games for Infants by A. Chitty, London: Paxton

Fingers and Thumbs by Ann Elliott, London: Stainer and Bell

*Follow my Leader (six beat and movement songs) by Mildred Logan, London: Paxton

Honey for Breakfast (twenty-four songs) by Joan Raeside, London: Chappell

*Listen to the Band (a first percussion book) by M. Cobby and I. M. Warner, London: Pitman

Movement and Song by Elizabeth Barnard, London: Curwen

*Music for the Nursery School by Linda Chesterman, London: Harrap

*Music Time by Mabel F. Wilson, London: Oxford University Press

My Book of Nature Songs by Vera Gray and Barbara Kluge, London: Oxford University Press

*New Nursery Jingles by Elizabeth Barnard, London: Curwen

*Nursery School Music Activities by Elizabeth Barnard, London: Curwen

On the Beat by Anne Mendoza and Joan Rimmer, London: Boosey and Hawkes

Oxford Book of Carols for Schools by Vaughan Williams and Shaw, London: Oxford University Press

★Ring-a-Ding Book 1 (and *Book 2*) by Yvonne Adair, London: Novello

★Seven (and *Seven More*) *Christmas Carols for Little Children* selected by Marjorie H. Greenfield, London: Curwen

Seven Movement Songs for the Nursery School by M. Anderson, London: Oxford University Press

★Seventy Simple Songs with Ostinati (accompaniments on several repeated notes) by Albert Chatterley, London: Novello

Simple Action Songs for the Nursery Class by Jennifer Day, London: Paxton

★Sing with Chimes by Olive Rees, London: Oxford University Press.

Six Action Songs for the Nursery Class by A. Chitty, London: Paxton

★Sixty (and *A Second Sixty*) *Songs for Little Children* by Whittaker, Wiseman and Wishart, London: Oxford University Press

Songs for the Nursery Class by Patricia Evans, London: Doric

The Children's First (*Second* and *Third*) *Christmas Book* (books of carols, songs, rhymes and games) by A. Chitty, London: Paxton

★The Clarendon Books of Singing Games 1 (and *11*) by Wiseman and Northcote, London: Oxford University Press

The First Book of Children's Play Songs by Robbins and Nordoff, published by Theodore Presser Company

The High Road of Song for Nursery School and Kindergarten Fletcher and Dennison, London: Warne

★The Oxford Nursery Song Book by Percy Buck, London: Oxford University Press

The Puffin Song Book by Leslie Woodgate, Harmondsworth: Penguin

Thirty (and *Thirty More*) *Folk Settings for Children* by Anne Mendoza and Joan Rimmer, London: Curwen

★Thirty Songs for the Nursery and Infant School by Winnifred E. Houghton, London: Boosey and Hawkes

★This Little Puffin (treasury of finger plays, singing and action games) by Elizabeth Matterson, Harmondsworth: Penguin

Tunes for the Music Makers by Olive Rees, London: Hohner

★Twenty Singing Activities for the Tinies by Nora Craig, London: Evans

What the Children Sing by Alfred Moffat, London: Stainer and Bell

Appendix 3 Books for children and teachers

Children's books

A Child's Book of Composers by Gordon Reynolds, London: Novello

A Child's Book of Instruments by Gordon Reynolds, London: Novello

Great Composers—Bach, Mozart, Beethoven Loughborough: Ladybird

Great Composers—Handel, Haydn, Schubert Loughborough: Ladybird

I Can Hear by Ronald Ridout, London: Purnell/ Bancroft

I Want to be a Musician by Carla Green, Edinburgh: W. and R. Chambers

Macdonald Starters—Music London: Macdonald

Musical Instruments Loughborough: Ladybird

Sounds and Music by Fice and Simkiss, Leeds: E. J. Arnold

Teachers' books

A Young Teacher's Guide to Class Music by Reynolds and Chatterley (1969) London: Novello
A teaching background to the class music lesson and a 'brush up' section for the lapsed music student.

An Introduction to Words and Music by I. Lawrence and P. Montgomery (1971) Harlow: Longman
A graded course in drama and music for junior schools offering many ideas to infant teachers, especially pupil book 1. Each chapter takes as a starting point the outline of a story which can form the core of some improvised drama which also provides opportunities for musical activities.

Children Make Music—Begin Making Music; Make Music; Making More Music by Richard Addison (1967) Edinburgh: Holmes McDougall
Pupil books full of musical experiments; they can give ideas to the nursery and infant teacher.

Creating Music with Children by Alice M. Snyder (1957) London: Mills Music
A personal account.

Creative Singing by Ken Evans (1971) London:
   Oxford University Press
An account of a fresh approach designed to develop
children's innate musical creativity by working through
their singing. Used successfully by musically untrained
teachers.

Discovering Music with Young Children by Eunice Bailey
   (1958) London: Methuen
A book based on some years' experimental work with
young children: a book about developing children and
their adventures in music.

Education Through Experience in the Infant School Years
   by Edna Mellor (1950) London: Basil Blackwell
Good useful reading for all educators of young children.

Explore and Discover Music by Mary Val Marsh (1970)
   London: Collier-Macmillan
An account of true classroom happenings documented
in detail, based on a creative approach to music
education.

Growing Up with Music by Mary Pape (1970) London:
   Oxford University Press
An informal account of the writer's experiences;
discussion of each year group, and of instruments.
Valuable reading for the infant teacher.

Listening and Moving by Winifred M. Carnie (1967)
   London: Nelson
A series of twenty lessons written for the nonspecialist
infant teacher. All the tunes referred to are notated and
good illustrations make this a practical little book.

Music and Young Children by Frances Aronoff (1969)
   London: Holt, Rinehart and Winston
Bases for young children's music education; processes of
musical growth; planning musical experiences and
examples; definitely a book for further reading.

Music Makers Stages 1–5 by Marion Berry (1973)
   Harlow: Longman
These are pupil books designed to help children with
the reading and writing of musical notation in a practical
way. Books 1 and 2 could be used with older or more
able reception children.

Music Movement and Mime for Children by Vera Gray
   and Rachel Percival (1962) London: Oxford University
   Press
A good background to the BBC broadcasts—is also full of
ideas and suggestions. Useful for continuous reference.

The Oxford School Music—Infant Book by J. P. B. Dobbs
   and W. Firth (1970) London: Oxford University Press
A good working basis for infant teachers; a detailed
book for the nonspecialist.

Appendix 4 Recorded material for children

There is much commercially recorded material available varying in suitability and musical standard. Many public libraries stock children's records if they have a record department and this is a good way of vetting a record before buying. Otherwise, browse in your local music shop, write for catalogues and ask your stockist to order if he does not stock the record.

Useful addresses
EMI Records, 33 Duke Street, London W1A 1ES

W. Paxton and Company Limited, 36-38 Dean Street, London W1V 6EP

Pye Records Limited, ATV House, Great Cumberland Place, London, W1A 1AG

Three Four Five Limited, 33 West Hill, London SW18 1RD

The British Association for Early Childhood Education, Montgomery Hall, The Oval, Kennington, London SE11 5SW.   (This organization has comprehensive lists of books, music and other publications relevant to the under fives.)

Useful records

Listen Move and Dance Numbers 1-3 HMV CLP 3762

Listen Move and Dance Number 4 HMV CLP 3531
Moving percussion and electronic sound pictures

Favourite Songs for Children by Michael Johns and
    Pat Whitmore RCA Victor SF 7911
Many nursery rhymes, Christmas songs attractively orchestrated and well sung.

Classical music
Children will listen to short snippets of almost any kind of music provided it is rhythmic or imaginative, and especially if you like it. Here is a short list which I am sure you can add to:

Debussy	*Claire de Lune*
	Golliwog's Cake-walk
	The Snow is Dancing
Delibes	*Coppelia*
Dukas	*Sorcerer's Apprentice*
Grieg	*Peer Gynt Suite: Morning; In the Hall of the Mountain King*

Haydn	*Toy Symphony*
Humperdinck	*Hansel and Gretel*
Ingelbrecht	*La Nursery*
Mendelssohn	*Fingal's Cave*
Prokofiev	*The Love of Three Oranges*
	Peter and the Wolf
Rimsky-Korsakov	*Flight of the Bumble-bee*
	Dance of the Tumblers
Rossini	*La Boutique Fantasque*
Saint-Saëns	*Carnival of the Animals*
Strauss	*Tritsch-Tratsch Polka*
	Radetzky March
Tchaikovsky	*Nutcracker Suite*—selections
	Swan Lake: Dance of the Little Swans
Vaughan Williams	*Fantasia on Greensleeves*
William Walton	*Facade*
Peter Worlock	*Capriol Suite*

Appendix 5 Notated songs

Baa Baa Black Sheep

Cock-a-doodle doo

or

Ding Dong Bell

Note: ♫ is three quavers in the time of two.

Down by the Station

78

Five Currant Buns

Five Currant Buns (alternate version)

Five Little Ducks

Five Little Froggies

J.G.

Here comes a Policeman

Hickory Dickory Dock

80

Hot Cross Buns

Hush-a-bye Baby

I Hear Thunder

F

81

In and Out the Windows

* Lower B

John Brown had a little Motor Car

Lavender's Blue

82

London's Burning

Looby (Lubin) Loo

Little Bo-Peep

Little Boy Blue

Mary Mary Quite Contrary

Mulberry Bush

Number One, Number One (This Old Man)

Oh dear! What can the matter be

* Lower B

One Little Brown Bird

One Finger, One Thumb Keep Moving

Paddling in the Puddles

* Lower B

Peas Pudding Hot

Peter Works with One Hammer

Polly put the Kettle On

87

Pray Open your Umbrella

Puffer Train

Pussy Cat, Pussy Cat, where have you been?

Mia – ow

88

See-saw Margery Daw

Skip to my Lou

Summer Goodbye

Sur le Pont d'Avignon

Ten Green Bottles (ten fat sausages)

Thank You for Giving me This Morning

90

The Muffin Man

There's a Hole in my Bucket

Three Blind Mice

Three Little Kittens

Mia - - ow   Mia - - ow

Train is a-coming

* Lower A   ♮ Lower G

We all Clap Hands Together

The Wheels on the Bus go Round and Round

Yankee Doodle

Index